Special Praise

"Memoirist Marcy Little's *Naked: My Body's Story* delivers the pleasures of the popular woman's self-help memoir genre while distinguishing itself in several meaningful ways. It tells the story of a woman's journey toward deeper self-awareness by using well-crafted storytelling to offer sustained, insightful reflection that extends beyond the narrative.

Little is immediately identifiably relatable. She is divorced. She fights with her mother at family gatherings. She has awkward run-ins with her ex-therapist. She likes it when her husband notices her body. Imagine your coolest, funniest, most-centered friend opening her heart to you over a luxurious, healthy meal, telling you stories that speak directly to your experiences of having a body that grows and breaks. That's *Naked: My Body's Story!*"

—Leah Shafer, PhD, Associate Professor of Media and
Culture Studies

"In *Naked: My Body's Story,* Marcy gives us a powerful roadmap to the healing that is possible when we as women own and share our stories, break free from the shame that keeps us stuck and feeling alone, and learn to fully embrace ourselves and our amazing bodies exactly as they are."

—Lorraine Faehndrich, Women's Pelvic Health and
Pain Relief Coach

"Marcy Little weaves a captivating story of love, redemption, longing, and forgiveness in the wake of intergenerational trauma."

—Melissa Tuckey, Author of *Tenuous Chapel* and Editor of
Ghost Fishing: An Eco-Justice Poetry Anthology

"An honest journey into the heart of healing. As a reader, you will vicariously walk this path toward wholeness with Marcy as your compassionate and loving guide."

—Rachel Bush, Licensed Ayurveda Practitioner and Certified Anusara Yoga Instructor

"I recently had the honor of reading the compelling *Naked: My Body's Story* by Marcy Little. As a psychiatrist who has worked in the fields of trauma and recovery from abuse for over twenty-five years, I found Marcy's story skillfully conveyed, moving, and filled with hope and humanity. Marcy brings a courageous willingness to look deeply at the impact of her childhood and adolescent traumatic experiences on her adult journey to find her own true freedom. Her memoir combines this deep honesty and vulnerability with an engaging writing style that allows the reader to really come to know her and her journey. This book was hard to put down! I feel enriched, both as a professional and as a woman in our objectifying culture, for having read her inspiring story."

—Kristen Nygren, MD

"*Naked* is raw, unapologetic, and relatable. Marcy's personal story does a service to other women who have survived trauma. Even with my background in psychology and human development, her account was a revelation. This honest and true chronicle of healing sexual abuse pushed me to my own edges, made me reflect on past traumas I thought I had resolved, and question their lasting impact on my body and in my relationships. Marcy's journey is in the living, and living can be messy. She doesn't pretend to have all the answers. Instead, with tremendous courage and vulnerability, she tells her story in a way we can all relate to, as fellow humans on the path to wholeness and integration. As we heal ourselves, so too do we heal this mixed-up world."

—Kathryn Caldwell, PhD

Naked

To my mother, my biggest hero, my greatest fan.

Table of Contents

Prologue

Can a fifteen-year-old virgin puking in the toilet because she's drunk give consent to a twenty-two-year-old man?

No.

No woman vomiting from intoxication can give consent. To this, add my premenstrual stage of development. I was a child on the cusp of blossoming into a young woman.

After I was raped, I became sexually promiscuous. It's in all the textbooks. Common behavior. But I wasn't reading any of these textbooks. I was just acting out my shame.

The die is cast. My body has been defiled. Any notion of innate worthiness, however small, I might have garnered in my childhood innocence has been stolen—cast aside permanently. Dirty laundry that's hopelessly stained.

I go with this new flow, engage in intercourse with teenage boys as clueless as I am. Moving through an unconscious cloud, I find myself secretly having sex with one of my sister's girlfriend's boyfriends. We break into my stepfather's small apartment during the day while he is at work, make toast and slice butter off the top of the stick instead of the front (a dead giveaway I have been there).

"Marcy, were you at my place yesterday?"

"Yeah. I just stopped in for a snack on my way into Binghamton," I lie.

While at my stepfather's place, my secret sex partner and I end up in the tub, naked, trying out things we heard about or saw in movies. Things that are supposed to be sexy.

I feel nothing. Nothing in my body. Nothing in my mind. Nothing in my heart. I am absent from the scene. Some other person has taken over my body and is going through the motions. Performing. Trying hard to be pleasing. Trying hard to be loved and accepted. Isn't this the way?

CB

It takes me thirty years to understand what happened to me. Thirty years to confront the pain encased in my cells. Thirty years to find my voice.

Like so many women, I am a survivor of sexual trauma and abuse. Like so many women, this early trauma still has a grasp on many aspects of my life, on many aspects of myself. Like so many women, I still struggle with intimacy and boundaries. Like so many women, things can still get really confusing in my body and my mind.

For a year, I studied myself, stayed with questions, listened deeply, and wrote it all down. An attempt to capture cellular level healing through a deep exploration of the contours of my own perplexing sexuality as a survivor of sexual trauma and abuse.

This is my journey.

Chapter One

And So It Begins . . .

"Do you remember how that babysitter touched us?" my sister casually asked.

We are sitting outside on my mother's front porch one halcyon day in early fall of 2016. On the hill across the river valley, leaves dress the trees with a mottled mix of rust and yellow and scarlet.

She takes a long drag off her Allegany Reservation cigarette.

"No. I don't," I say as my head, now searching for that lost memory, surveys the scene.

"I guess you wouldn't. I was only three," she replies and takes another long slow drag of her cigarette.

I choke on my spit.

For as long as I can remember, I have been aware of the sexual part of my human nature. It seems like that awareness was present from an early age, though I couldn't say exactly when. I just *knew* it was there. It was a part of me.

My sister is two years older than me. If she was three, then I was one. Of course, I have no conscious memory of it—but my body does.

Denny continues to smoke in the slow lazy way she has, while my diaphragm spasms in a struggle to remove the offending spit from my lungs. My mind is cataloging every time my body has recoiled in fear when my partner touches me with desire.

1

Bessel Van der Kolk in his seminal book, *The Body Keeps the Score*, cautions that "Long after a traumatic experience is over, it may be reactivated at the slightest hint of danger."

The earth opens beneath me. I fall in.

The rest of the day is a blur of overcooked hamburgers and family bickering. I sneak sideways glances at my mother wondering, *How could you let this happen to us?*

ೞ

The following Saturday, I am sitting with some of my African dance friends. We have come together to have a girls' night and make body butter. I've brought enough beeswax for three gallons of lotion. We sit on the carpeted floor of the small apartment sharing a joint while a woman I've met for the first time works away in the kitchen. The wooden spoon swipes against the side of the melting pot.

I share the story my sister told me. I feel nothing as I talk.

"It confirms something for me," I say. "Something I've always known but could never put into words. It explains so much."

According to Van der Kolk, trauma, by nature, shuts down the limbic and neocortical parts of the brain that allow us to give words to our experience. Instead, the brain stem, the part that induces us to fight, run, or freeze when our lives are in danger, is activated. Even if my initial trauma had been at a later age, I might not have been able to put it into words.

My friends look at me with compassion. Soon, they are hugging me, patting me on the back. No tears come.

Another woman speaks up.

"I was sexually abused by my stepfather."

This fellow African dancer's lack of boundaries has grated against my psyche since we first met. When Marisa hugs, she gives what I call a "vagina hug," pressing her whole body into mine, her crotch onto my leg. I try to relax when she does this. *Be cool. Go with the flow.* But I hate it. When she dances behind me in class, she doesn't keep space between our bodies. By the time I have reached the end of the floor, ready to make my exit dance move to the drummers, I can feel her breath on my back. I turn around, motion for her to back up, but within minutes, she's right behind me coming down the floor again. *Does she even see my body in front of her?*

Marisa recounts the years of violation she endured at the hands of a father figure.

"I'm okay with it," she says, "I think it's just a part of me now. My sexuality is alive in everything I do." She blinks twice to convince herself that what she has just said is as normal as making body salve with the girls.

A softness rises up in my chest toward this woman, who, like me, is doing the very best she can.

K

My first orgasm surprised me during a daily afternoon nap when I was three. I had the habit of pulling the covers together and putting them between my legs where I would rub against them. It soothed me and helped me fall asleep. One day this nap-time ritual caused an overwhelmingly pleasurable sensation.

What was that? I wondered as I went about trying to make it happen again. And again. And again. Sometimes I succeeded, many times I did not. There was some mystery in it I couldn't fully understand.

Somehow I knew that what was happening was private; that it was just for me. I began to look forward to these special times with myself during the day or at night.

At age four, I had my first sleep over at my friend Laura's house. I loved Laura. I especially loved that she lived within walking distance of my house.

I was startled when her mother said we'd be sleeping in the same bed.

In the same bed? I thought.

But our bodies will be so close.

I didn't sleep a wink that night, aware all night long of Laura's skin so near to my own. Would we touch each other? Would someone know? My cheeks glowed in the dark with shame and excitement. I had no idea where this shame or desire came from at that time. Now, as I look back, I can see how much of my future sexual terrain had already been set. Was it the improper and unwanted touch of the male babysitter when I was a baby or was there something more? How much of the hurt in my mother's sexually abused body was living actively in my own, causing feelings to arise that I had no conscious context to understand?

My mother once allowed a neighbor's child to babysit for me when I was just a baby. She came home to find me covered in bruises. Unable to protect us as she had been unable to protect herself growing up, she allowed that child to babysit for me again.

Later, she called me an "independent" child.

"When you were tired, you would just go fall asleep under the picnic table. We would find you there after all the guests had gone home."

I learned to crawl to safety and stay out of sight even before I learned to walk.

༄

We moved from our sheltered neighborhood in Rockville, MD, into our new suburban home in Pittsford, NY, when I was five. Our dog, Muffit, was a small, scrappy Tibetan-terrier with scruffy white fur that got dirty easily.

There were lots of young children to play with in our new white upper-middle-class neighborhood. Kids on bikes at all hours of the day.

I had made some friends who would come over periodically for snacks and to share my Barbies.

In the process of moving in, a rolled-up carpet was left leaning at an angle against the wall of our living room. Muffit made it her lover. She would hump the hell out of that carpet roll while Denny and I watched television.

At first, we pretended it wasn't happening. It seemed so private. My mother would shoo her away. "Muffit. Stop that."

Muffit would slink dejectedly into the kitchen, but it wasn't long before she was back at the carpet roll.

I was mesmerized. As Muffit humped away, my cheeks reddened. Isn't this what I did alone at night with my sheets and pillows? Everyone who saw Muffit found it shameful. Did this make my relationship with the bunched sheets equally shameful?

My sister and I giggled when Muffit started. When our friends came over, we showed off Muffit like a circus act. We all stood watching as her little bottom moved up and down, up and down. We looked at each other wondering how this could be happening. It was exhilarating and embarrassing.

Muffit became more and more emphatic in her lovemaking to the carpet roll. She started to growl at us if we stepped too near, making the boundaries of her pleasure clear. One day, she bit one of my friends. Broke the skin. That was the end. My mother gave Muffit away to a family in the country where she would be more happy and less dangerous to the neighborhood children. The carpet went, too. I don't remember where, but it disappeared along with the dog.

ᛒ

My sister had also discovered the secret pleasures housed between her legs. I would often end up in her room at some point in the night when we were young. In matching twin beds, we played the game "What's

Up?" where we each took turns hiding under the covers and sticking some part of our body up into the sheet. It was the other's job to identify and name which body part was at play. We could play this game for hours, never tiring of it.

One night, two years after my secret discovery, she let me in on her own.

"Do you touch yourself *there*?" she asked.

I knew what she meant, but played as if I didn't.

"Where?"

"You know. There," and she pointed to the space between her seven-year-old thighs.

I desperately wanted to tell my sister what I had discovered. To add to my already increasing shame, I think my mom was onto me because my crotch was rubbed raw. She would put Vaseline on it at night before I went to bed. I couldn't bring myself to divulge my secret—to my sister and, especially, to my mom. I didn't dare. Something held me back. If I told my sister what I did, would she make fun of me? If I told my mom, would she think I was a freak or think I was being nasty? Would she tell me, "Marcy, stop that!" like she did with Muffit. Would she send me away, too?

Girls were supposed to *touch* themselves to find pleasure, not rub on a sheet.

Why did I even know this at the age of five?

"No," I said to my sister, "I don't."

Our nighttime game of "What's Up," never felt the same again. We were different. My sister's sexuality was normal. Mine was not.

Around this same time, we had a twelve-year-old female babysitter. She came around during the daytime, probably so that my mother could do the grocery shopping in peace. In the living room, still charged with poor Muffit's sexual energy, was a feather duster. The babysitter, my sister, and I would make up imaginative play with this yellow-tipped feather duster. I have no idea who thought up the game, but before long we were taking off our clothes while we tickled each other's private parts with it.

It was titillating. It was wrong. We knew we would be in trouble if we got caught. We did it anyway. The risk only enhanced the thrill of it all. Somewhere in the back of my mind I wondered, *Is this okay?*

I enjoyed it even while it didn't feel quite right.

We were children. I wanted to play the game, which is why it never occurred to me until much, much later in my life, that what went down in that living room on sunny afternoons with the babysitter was a violation. There was no one there to set the boundaries. To keep us safe. To protect our innocence.

Our twelve-year-old feather duster lover wasn't our only babysitter. My mother also paid a male teenager to take care of us whenever she and my dad went out. One day, I spied Denny in her bedroom with him. He was reading her a book. Her legs were wide-open exposing her underwear.

Close your legs! my mind screamed. I saw my seven-year-old sister's open legs as an invitation and no one for miles to protect her.

☃

I was a child who loved to play with my Barbies, ride my bike whenever I could, play make-believe games with my sister and the other neighborhood kids, and tried to keep thoughts of my sexual awakening to when I was alone in my bed at night. I didn't know my parents' marriage was unraveling. I didn't know my mother was in therapy or that she had begun to scratch the surface of her own painful story of sexual abuse at the hands of her father—an alcoholic and extremely traumatized WWII vet. I didn't know that the Gung Fu lessons she was taking three times a week were giving her the power to leave an unhappy, oppressive marriage. I didn't know until later that my father had also raped my mother when she refused him one night in bed.

Our house was infused with Marine Corps strictness. My father, also an extremely traumatized vet (Vietnam), was shot through the head three months into his deployment and miraculously survived. Proud to have served his country, he bore the deafness in his right ear like a badge of honor. The nightmares and post-traumatic stress were kept very secret.

His father, District Attorney and later, ruthless judge of a large city in upstate NY, had no patience for my father's artistic, sensitive side. He taught him to pull himself up by the bootstraps by sadistically making him dig and refill holes all day in the lawn on his only day off. Any lingering signs of weakness were beaten out of him at the dinner table each night with the belt from my grandfather's waist while his older brother, younger sister, and mother watched, pretending not to be horrified.

I believe my mother was every bit as scared of my father as we were. He carried the law and his word was gospel. Any divergence from the house rules would find us bending over, grabbing our ankles while he stood behind us as we waited for his heavy hand. When the slap came, I would wet my pants, do a forward roll and cry, humiliated to the core. My sister, older and closer to my father, weathered it better. Before long, my sister and I became allies against his rageful discipline. One day, when our father took his military stance as he prepared to hit us, we grabbed our ankles, looked at each other, and giggled. He never hit us again.

∞

What I did not yet have the capacity to understand or put into words began to show up as nightmares while I was still awake. My bedroom, at the back side of the upstairs of the new house, looked out onto a hill where new construction was taking place. Pine trees stood at the edge of where the earth had been churned up. Its loamy smell penetrated my room. In the darkness of the night, I watched the silhouette of the trees. One night, they began to move. They walked toward our house, moving ominously toward my bedroom.

Most children, when scared at night, run for the comfort of their mother. I did not. I was terrified of my parents' bedroom, scared I would anger my father. I laid there, frozen, petrified, shaking, willing the trees to stop, but they just kept coming. I knew I would be consumed. I closed my eyes and trembled until I finally fell asleep.

I began staring at the ceiling before turning out the lights, focusing my mind on one spot to make it open up. *Was I trying to create a safe space to escape into?* I believed that if I concentrated hard enough, I could make objects move at my will or even disappear. How else could I stop those trees from coming to get me? At some point, the fear of being devoured by the trees must have been stronger than the fear of disturbing my father at night. I must have told them about the trees because my parents changed my room. My new room was much smaller at the front of the house facing the street. A street lamp kept it partially lit throughout the night, and the trees, now out of sight, disappeared from my consciousness.

೮೮

It is April 2017, and I am on my way back from a journey to Mexico. Pulled out of work by my doctor for a severe reaction to mold in the classroom at the school where I teach, I headed to one of my favorite healing spots on the planet—Maya Tulum on the Yucatan Peninsula. After a week of relaxation on the white sands of the Riviera Maya, Mayan shamanic healing sessions, and midnight margaritas with new friends, I am headed home with an immune system reboot.

I have made my way to the gate of my connecting flight in Philly. I don't know why I am feeling so tired. I have just had the time of my life in Tulum. I am fully rested. Tan. Radiant. Renewed.

I am walking the long walk to Terminal F where I will catch my puddle jumper home to Ithaca. All along the way there are signs for ground transport. I stoically ignore them all.

I will walk, I confirm to myself. *The exercise will do me good.*

As I approach Terminal F, I marvel at the weariness in my legs. Why am I so exhausted? By the time I arrive at my gate, I can't wait to sit down. My backpack, I realize, is loaded with everything that would no longer fit in my carry-on, which is now crammed with Talavera style hand-painted Mexican pottery. It slowly dawns on me that I've been carrying fifty-two pounds of ceramics on my back and pushing everything I brought to Mexico for more than a mile.

No wonder I am tired. I think to myself. This old pattern of determination and self-discipline handed down the ranks perhaps from even further back than my father's father, a long outdated family trait, kicks me to the curb sometimes. *We do it to ourselves*, I think. *Aren't we our own worst enemies?*

I see this resistant, outmoded pattern loud and clear, and smile knowingly at myself. Yet, there is something I don't see. Is it just the Talavera in my bag that is weighing me down?

༄

My husband, Chris, shifts back and forth, moving in and out of my sight. I see him as I roll my carry-on down the ramp of our small Ithaca airport.

He is wearing the rust-colored jeans I bought him at the Monoprix on the Champs-Élysée in Paris so many years back.

Damn you look good, I think as I move through the swinging gate into the center of the tiny Ithaca airport. I recall our first months, years together, when just the sight of him would bring a rush of excitement to my loins. The skin of his face and neck is a shade pinker than his pants, despite the frequent applications of the SPF 50 sunscreen he uses dutifully.

Full body hug. Soft. Familiar. Delicious.

My hand on his hip, then butt cheek in the middle of the mostly deserted airport. It is 10:34 p.m. I can feel the steely gaze of the woman seated to our right. I don't care. His hug feels like home and I sink right into it.

"You look good," I say as I size him up. "I like your pants."

We are both beaming.

"You too," he says, words stick in his mouth with unrehearsed emotion.

He puts on the heavy backpack I've been wearing most of the day on my trek back.

"What have you got in here? A dead body?"

I just smile as he pushes my carry-on in front of us. We walk out of the airport hand in hand greedily stealing mutual glances.

And then it happens.

He places his hand on my back as we are crossing the road to the parking lot and my body doesn't want it there.

In the car, he places his hand on my knee and my body doesn't want it there.

Shit, I think. *Here we go again. Did it have to happen so soon?*

I gently move my knee away to free it once again. To free myself once again.

The easy openness I felt upon first seeing Chris has been swallowed whole, disappeared into a dark and mysterious vortex of history. I long for its return. I long for my own receptivity to his touch, but it is nowhere to be found.

"It will take some time for me to get back," I say into the dark hum of the night.

"I know," he says.

Chapter Two

Foundation

Chris and I have been a couple for over fifteen years. Our paths converged over butter at our local supermarket one chilly October afternoon in 2002. I was in the middle of an unsalvageable rough spot in my first marriage and Chris's late wife, who died of cancer, had been gone just a year.

We first met in 1990, when I was working with his late wife Cheryl in the ESL department of the local high school. I was saddened to learn of Cheryl's cancer and had attended her memorial service where I found Chris to be beautiful in the expression of his deep love and devotion to Cheryl for over twenty-four years.

"I fell in love with Cheryl first," he said to the people who had gathered. "I spent the next few years convincing her she loved me, too."

A year earlier, at our local food Coop, while Cheryl was fighting for her life, I spied him across the parking lot. Still living the uncertainty of my own marriage, I was surprised when I heard an inner voice say loud and clear, "You will marry this man."

A year after Cheryl's death, I hug him while his developmentally disabled eleven-year-old daughter Lillian sits in the shopping cart talking to strangers. The air thins. My head spins. My heart explodes open. I feel as though I might faint.

"We should get our kids together," he says as he gives me his phone number.

I teeter away wondering what the hell just happened.

The next day, he calls.

Soon, we are caught up in a love affair. Not sure I am ready to leave my marriage, though the uncertainty of the foundation of our union grows more apparent each day; Chris and I meet in secret for months. Our connection is electric; our thirst for each other unquenchable.

The first few years of our coupling are intense. We ride the raging hormone-induced state fully alive. Hot. Ready. Do I ever once say no to sex during those years of endorphin overload? I do not. I don't want to. It is wonderful.

"I just hope someday you'll become friends," says Margerie, Chris's mother, on my first visit to meet her. It is the third year of our relationship, and we still can't keep our hands off each other.

After my divorce from my first husband is complete, a house thirty feet from my front door at Ecovillage goes up for sale. It is the largest home in the neighborhood, and the only one that could eventually accommodate our two families coming together. Head over heels in love, I ask Chris to buy the house.

Now, living thirty feet apart in separate homes, Chris comes over to make me coffee and give me a kiss while I'm still in bed. At night, after our kids are asleep, we snuggle until I dose off. Once I'm asleep, he goes home to finish out the night. On the weekends, we blend our families over brunch in one of our houses. We find a rhythm of distance and togetherness that keeps our bliss intact. We get married and for a year, we keep up this dance.

Then we start living together.

And things get a bit more complicated.

What we each bring to the "living together" table isn't going to be easy. I bring my son Zain, twelve years old, born with the progressive muscle wasting disease, Duchenne muscular dystrophy. Zain has just recently begun using a wheelchair full time. Chris brings his seventeen-going-on-six-year-old daughter with developmental and cognitive disabilities, Lillian, who still wears pull-ups to bed and wakes her dad several times a night.

Our hands are full. We are carrying a LOT together—precisely why living in separate houses thirty feet apart, even after our first year of marriage, seemed so appealing at the time. We decide it's time to move in together when Zain can no longer make the short walk from the front door of the house to the car.

I sell my house and use the money I make off the sale to pay for an addition on the back of Chris's house, an addition that will house an Endless Pool with a hydraulic lift chair, where Zain will be able to get exercise daily to preserve muscle, lung, and heart function.

The good news? We work well as a team. We complement each other. Chris is patient and endlessly giving to the needs of both of our kids. I provide much needed boundaries to Lillian and a degree of emotional intelligence to most situations.

Early on in the relationship, we attend a workshop for blended families. The workshop leader, Elizabeth Einstein, an expert in stepfamily relations, beseeches all the couples in the workshop to "make your marriage primary."

"In blended families, the children will do everything in their power to pull you apart. You must be sure to keep your couple at the center," she says. "Every week, you go on a date. Once a month, you get away overnight. Once a year you go away for at least a week."

Though some members of Chris's family find it selfish, we take her words to heart and do as she says. It's a good thing we do because it works. Over fifteen years later, we are still together. Still going on weekly dates. Still getting out of town together, albeit less frequently. Still going somewhere new every summer for over a week.

Alas, now living together, sharing the bathroom, dirty counters, wet pull-ups, and wheelchairs, the hormones start to fade. Without the buzz of our attraction or the hormones to keep my body open to my man, a deeper voice in my body starts to speak. My history of sexual trauma begins to show up with growing frequency. Small gestures, once welcome, now trigger old fears.

Things have begun to get a lot more real.

os

The rape happened at the end of my sophomore year in high school. A friend's older boyfriend was having a party at his small, decrepit house off Route 17. There was a keg of Genesee Light, red plastic cups, and a mix of over- and underage drinkers. I don't remember much about that party except that at some point, my friend Katrina told me that her sister's ex-boyfriend, Sylvan, thought I was cute.

I was fifteen years old. I barely had breasts much less pubic hair. A late bloomer and a long-distance runner, my body was decidedly behind that of my peers. It would be at least three more months before I would begin menstruating and, even then, it came sporadically until I turned twenty-one.

I don't recall how much I had already had to drink that night or if I had smoked marijuana or ingested other substances floating around the outdoor party, but Katrina's comment piqued my interest. Sylvan was twenty-two years old and had been going out with her sister for years. They were in an "off" period, which meant that Sylvan had the right to go looking elsewhere. Why he was looking at me I still can't fathom, but he was. And to some starving part of my soul, that look felt good.

We went home together from the party. Well, not home exactly, rather to Katrina's boyfriend's house. Sylvan and I found our way to a full-size bed in the same room as Katrina and her boyfriend. We all made out together on opposite sides of the room for a while. Eventually, they left the room to go bunk somewhere else, leaving Sylvan and me alone.

Needless to say, I was a virgin.

I was also drunk. You know, blotto, hammered, three-sheets-to-the-wind drunk.

Twice, as we were fooling around, I got up to throw up. The second time, Sylvan came to check on me.

"Are you alright?" he asked through the door as I wiped puke from the corners of my mouth.

"Yes, I'm fine," I lied. My head was spinning so hard I had to hold the walls as I made my way back down the dark hallway to the even darker room. I don't remember much of what happened in the bed that night, but I do believe I thought I wanted it at the time. I'm pretty sure he went down on me, though I don't remember feeling anything. He definitely penetrated me and called out my name when he came.

In the morning, he was on top of me again. I didn't say stop. Didn't ask him to get off me. I just waited for him to finish, shrinking inside, becoming one with the wallpaper.

It hurt, and I wasn't drunk anymore. I had full cognizance of what was taking place.

I expected there would be a lot of blood on the sheets like in the movies. But there was no sign of a broken hymen or anything of the sort. Just a shameful wet spot where my bottom had just been when I got up.

I let Sylvan know that he was my first. That until this encounter, I had been a virgin. I doubt he even knew how old I was. Or maybe he did. He seemed surprised to find out that I had never slept with anyone before. He furrowed his brow and said, "Sorry."

I got into the car that would take me home. As soon as I was inside, sitting safely behind the backdoor window, I began to wonder what had just happened. Sylvan stood in the paved drive and watched as the car pulled away. I couldn't make myself greet his glance.

When I got home, everyone in the house was still sleeping. I crept silently up the stairs, took off my clothes and got into the shower. I stayed in that shower a long time. I used half a bar of soap to wash the night and early morning off my skin. I got into bed more dishonored and alone than ever before. I already knew I could never tell anyone about what had just happened. I kept Sylvan and my secret closeted in my heart for many years to come.

One day, almost two decades later, I heard someone use the words "statutory rape." My ears perked up. For the first time it occurred to me that what had happened that night could be considered rape. I had always felt guilty. Surely I was the culpable one. Hadn't I wanted it? Wasn't I curious?

I tried the words on. *Statutory rape.* I didn't use them in conversation to describe what had happened to me until I was well into my thirties. It was still a phrase to describe other people's experience. Every time I said it, I felt like an impostor. I kept on saying it though, and gradually, over time, I began to believe it. I added myself to the long list of women whose bodies had been violated, though my experience seemed insignificant compared to so many others. He didn't take me at gunpoint. Didn't kick me down and spread my legs with a knife to my neck. His friends didn't hold me down on a pool table in the back of a bar and take turns, then leave me in a heap next to a dumpster behind the building. He thought I was cute. He asked to take me home.

And I said yes.

In some states, the age of consent is thirteen. All states but three legally acknowledge consent at the age of eighteen. At fifteen, I was still very much a girl wishing she were a woman. Drunk, I was even less legally capable of offering myself to a twenty-two-year-old male.

Claude Halmos, French psychoanalyst and author of *Pourquoi l'amour ne suffit pas*, (*Why Love Isn't Enough*) and *Grandir*, (*Growing Up*), explains in her monthly column in the French periodical *Psychologies* why Hélène, a twenty-year-old from Lyon, couldn't resist the advances of an older man when she was sixteen. Halmos explains that a girl of sixteen is still a "grand-adolescent," and "legally a minor." An older man has the duty to behave responsibly, to protect the minor where the power situation is totally unequal:

> " . . . a girl of sixteen, inexperienced, is naturally
> perturbed by the desire she inspires in an older man.
> And this allows him—who is not perturbed in the least
> and knows exactly what he's doing—to take advantage
> of her."

Halmos emphatically denies that a sixteen-year-old girl can give consent to an older man. It is, she says "indeed a form of rape, imposed not by physical force, but by pressure, a psychological hold."

For many years following this experience, I allowed my body to be used like a disposable toy. A young man's interest was enough for me to feel he had some predetermined right to do as he wished. I asked for so little in return.

I didn't know I was perpetuating the harm that had been done to me as a child and didn't understand that I had deeply internalized the belief that my body was made to be despoiled by men. The guys I hooked up with didn't know it either.

My best friend in high school was also sexually active. But she enjoyed it. This was clear and upsetting to me. As we shared stories of our sex lives, I would puff up my chest and recount the tales, never letting on that I simply didn't get it. What was all the hype about? As Kayla talked, I listened, mesmerized.

He did what? I would think. *And you liked it? In the car? How many times?*

Kayla was a dancer and had a well-developed, intimate relationship with her body. I was a long-distance runner, accustomed to pushing through pain to get to the finish line. And this is what I did in every single sexual encounter for the next three years.

The summer of my eighteenth year, I decided I wanted more. I was ready to know what all the fuss was about because I sure wasn't getting it. I had finally reached the age of consent. How interesting that I wanted to start having the kind of experience I could truly consent to. I wanted what Kayla had. I wanted to enjoy sex, feel *something*, but I had no idea how. I had a summer fling with a family friend. We were living in a cockroach-infested basement apartment in downtown Albany for the summer, working on a cruise boat on the Hudson.

Terrance was tall, smart, and loved women.

This will be a good place to start, I thought.

Wrong. Old habits (if you can call them old at this point in a young person's life), die hard. Again, I found myself skillfully seducing this young man, taking pride in his pleasure while still absent to my own.

My freshman year in college, I fell into a relationship with a senior on the same floor of my dorm. Jerry was tall, skinny, and 100 percent inoffensive. He taught me to play backgammon. His roommate, who loved the Beastie Boys, taught me to throw a football with a mean spiral. We all spent tons of time together.

Jerry and I would find ourselves alone in his dorm room. We would cuddle and nap, but I couldn't bring myself to have sex with him. I couldn't fully let him in. Not to my body—this war-torn land that hadn't a clue how to share intimacy. I said no all year long, causing Jerry an inordinate amount of frustration. Even when we visited his home in Connecticut to attend his sister's wedding, I said no.

I didn't know why I couldn't let him in. I didn't understand what was wrong with me.

Years later, I got a clue. I was reading *Belle de Jour*, the story of a woman who, molested as a young child, could not open her body to her loving husband. His tender acceptance of her did not mirror the intense shame and loathing she felt for herself. Instead, she found her sexual opening and pleasure in a brothel where she submitted to rough men who dominated and raped her. The author of this book, Joseph Kessel, whose main character was later played by Catherine Deneuve in an eponymous film, somehow understood the tormented psyche of a sexually abused woman.

Jerry had become a friend. A person I trusted. Someone I knew would never hurt me. The realms of trust and sexuality were fractured, not to intermingle lest the thick of my wounds come to the surface.

A child who is protected, whose innocence remains intact until she is developmentally prepared to explore the erotic with others, will most likely go on to enjoy the unfolding of the pleasures of the body. This is Kayla's story.

A child whose physical, emotional, and/or sexual boundaries are violated will struggle. Perhaps even for her whole life. When this happens, on the most basic level, the message reverberates through her body: the world is not safe. Fundamental trust has been broken, damaged, even destroyed. This is my story.

Was Sylvan guilty? Was I? Once I got used to using the word rape to describe my first sexual encounter, I toyed with the idea of talking to someone about what had happened the first time I had sex and of looking to hold Sylvan accountable. Too much time had elapsed for justice, but I imagined what would happen if I were ever to confront Sylvan as an adult. To use the word rape in his presence. *Statutory rape.*

Sylvan went on to marry Katrina's sister. Did he ever think of me and that fateful night again? Or was it just one of many nights when he exploited underage female strangers while he and his girlfriend were "taking a break?" Did he carry even an inkling of guilt or remorse beyond the morning light? Or, unlike me, was he able to wash it all off in the shower the next day? Did the memory of the drunk fifteen-year-old virgin he deflowered creep in years later when he was shaving or while he raked fall leaves into a pile for his daughters to jump into or when he dropped off his oldest daughter at her boyfriend's house for the first time? Did he ever give a second thought to what that night might have done to the fifteen-year-old girl he never saw again? To the impact it might have had on her identity or how it would influence her relationship to her sexual body for so many years to come?

03

"How young were you when it happened?"

I am sitting across from Joel, my new therapist. He was recommended by a good friend while I was in the throes of healing from the devastating health consequences of being exposed to mold and leaving the workplace where I had become sick.

An electric current runs strongly through his body up into his third eye. I see it. I feel it. At first, I thought he needed to relax but now I see that he is just fiercely awake. Deeply alive. He is a Zen Buddhist Master. His counsel has grown from a life immersed in practice and service to his community.

"It happened before I can consciously remember."

I don't squirm in my chair, start to fiddle with something, or pull lint from my shirt. I look him right in the eyes while inside I wonder how he will react. Though there is nothing new about this fact for me, it still feels new to say out loud.

"But there were many times after that that I do remember. It became sort of a theme in my life."

He nods and waits.

Joel's specialty is grief therapy. He worked as a counselor and head of the local Hospice for almost thirty years, helping people navigate the pain of loss—the loss of loved ones, the loss of identity, the loss of one's own life.

The moment I sit down in his chair each week, my eyes begin to prick with hot tears. It's as if the chair holds the energy of every client who has ever sat here and let their sadness flow. The armrests hold me like a hug. The soft cushion underneath me is an open heart to sink into. A safe place to feel. I have come to surrender, but am still surprised when the salty tears roll down my cheeks and my belly convulses instinctively. A crust that houses my old sadness cracks open while I cry. I don't hold it back. I don't want to.

"That's it. Just let that pain come."

It is formless. It is nameless sadness, and my body opens to the expression of a nebulous hurt. Waves of grief rise up and exit through my mouth. My exhale is an audible surge of wind, hot and full.

"Now feel the chair beneath you. Your arms on the armrests."

Joel regularly interrupts my flow to bring me back to the present. It disturbs me, especially when I'm in the midst of a good story. But I try to yield every time. I have put myself in his skilled hands, after all. I have asked him to help lead me toward wholeness.

I breathe and do as he says. When the tears slow, I open my eyes. He is looking straight at me.

"I think it's important to name the quest you're on, beyond this terrible hurt."

The quest I'm on beyond this terrible hurt?

I sit with that for a moment.

"You are both the wound and the Quan Yin," Joel says.

I grimace.

"What is that face about?" he asks.

"That feels hard," I say.

"It *is* hard."

It is hard to be both the wounded child and the loving mother who has to hold her, I think.

Quan Yin, Buddhist deity of Compassion, hangs in my yoga/meditation/writing room. She is painted on a scarlet-colored silk scarf made by hand in Indonesia. I bought it one day many years ago when a visitor to Ecovillage at Ithaca, where I live, opened her suitcase. Full of beautiful things she'd brought back from her recent trip to Bali, Quan Yin poured herself onto the table. The moment I laid eyes upon her I wanted her for myself. I needed her. Maybe she needed me, too.

I snatched her off the table, afraid that if I waited a moment longer, a neighbor might do the same.

"How much?"

The long scarf drapes over the end of the tall wooden bookcase near the door of the well-used room where I meditate, practice yoga, study, and write. I look at her as I write this now. I see that her gaze has welcomed and watched over me each time I have entered for the past twenty years. While her grace has permeated my practice over the years, I see that I still need to turn her power and wisdom inward toward myself.

She stands on a lotus in full bloom, one hand outstretched holding a vase-like vessel. Her other hand is raised in a *shuni* (patience) mudra over her heart. It holds the long stem of a green plant with five leaves at its end. Her face is soft and peaceful. There is a small dot over her third eye. This Buddhist goddess of mercy, bodhisattva of compassion, stands regally on her lotus, reigning her benevolent grace on all who worship her. (And those who don't.)

Joel doesn't ask me for specifics. He doesn't ask to hear my story of abuse. Instead he says, "You would be even if this terrible thing hadn't happened to you."

"I would be what? Sexually abused?"

He nods holding my gaze with searing intensity.

"Every time a woman is seen as an object, she is sexually abused. Maybe not to the same degree, but it's still the same thing." I absorb this statement as I inhale.

When I share this with my friend Han, she objects.

"Every time a man's gaze comes to our bodies and sees our form, sees us as an object to be lusted after and desired, we are hurt? What about our animal nature?"

Han has never been directly sexually abused.

I sit with Joel's assertion and Han's question. It becomes clear that the *problem* of seeing women solely as our bodies, the problem of being seen merely as meat or an object of desire, has everything to do with our shared history. The overarching systems of oppression. The historical ownership of women's bodies makes being seen as an object today problematic. We all share this common legacy, a legacy that leaves us gasping in the struggle to restore, protect, and maintain our humanity.

"Yes, we are animals," Joel says when I bring it up at our next session. "And this can be a beautiful thing, this pleasure of the flesh for flesh. The problem arises when we lose sight of the other as *Mystery*. When we share ourselves as pure objects, we fail to acknowledge the inherent mystery of who and what we are."

Spoken like a true Zen master.

"Yes," I agree, though I don't yet fully understand what he means.

CB

Like so many women, it took a long time for me to admit to myself that I was sexually abused. Even as I write these words, some part of me wants to deny it is true. Is it because my mother's experience of incest loomed so large over our lives growing up that the violations against my own body seemed insignificant? Is it that some part of me felt excited, curious, and naughty the times my babysitters touched me inappropriately? Is it that I have never wanted to see myself as a victim? Is it that I fear I may get lost in the self-contempt that inevitably goes along with this sort of violation?

Most children of sexual abuse believe deep down they did something to cause it, and thus deserve what happened to them as well as the subsequent feelings of shame associated with their sexuality. What child who is sexually abused is not left with the sense that there is something inherently wrong with him or her? The secret, kept hidden over time, causes the personality to maneuver and lie to itself to cover up this badness. This stain. This dark mark. This truth. This certainty of one's fundamental failing. This hidden disorder that makes one different.

Or so I have always felt, thought, believed, was certain, I exemplified.

ଔ

Soon after Chris and I start living together, I bring it up. Gently at first.

"When you look at my breasts like that, it makes me feel uncomfortable."

"Why? I just love your breasts."

"Because it makes me feel like an object."

This makes no sense to him. So, I tell him the story of when I was fifteen—drunk and a virgin—and raped at a high school party by a twenty-two-year-old man. I tell him about the babysitters, the young man who jerked off in front of my best friend and me when we were ten years old changing into our bathing suits at a hippy music festival in upstate NY, the man in a parked car who called us over and exposed his penis to us. The list gets very long.

Chris cries when he hears these stories. But how can he know the way they have affected my ability to give and receive love? My ability to open and share my heart with ease? Even I don't fully understand it. But I know that I am still, at least partially, a prisoner of my past. A victim of what happened to me, my mother, my sister, and so many women in the world around me.

My husband is a sensitive, loving man, who truly has never wished to hurt me.

Truly.

But he does.

We do.

For years.

Unknowingly.

Unintentionally.

And then I come home cracked open from Tulum, Mexico, and I say, "Enough."

Chapter Three

Awakening

When the sacred vessel of our childhood body has been violated, when primal and necessary boundaries have not been honored by those entrusted with our care, when the silent *no* we scream from within is not heard or heeded, something breaks. Wordless, it reverberates off walls not fully constructed.

☙

I get sick from exposure to mold. Twice. Both times from my sacred teaching space—the classroom I teach in every day. The room in which young minds and hearts get nourished by nasal vowels, French grammar, vocabulary and culture, and my sometimes-off-the-wall stories.

I get sick.

I get terribly sick.

The road to recovery is long. As the inhalers, Prednisone, nebulizers, raw food diet, sleep, sleep, and more sleep gradually calm my sick cough, headaches, mental fog, body aches, suicidal depression, and extreme exhaustion, I try going back to the classroom. It doesn't work. Even in the newest part of the building, my symptoms return within twenty minutes of teaching. Microscopic mold spores, once released into the environment, travel on every surface: students' clothes, hair, backpacks. I have become highly sensitized to the air in the entire school.

They find the source of the mold. The nighttime janitorial staff has been leaving the water tube just outside the floor basin where it drips all night onto the floor. Mold has grown unseen on the wooden bookshelf built into the wall of my room adjacent to the janitor's closet. They shut down the classroom until remediation could occur. But, for me, the damage to my health is done.

The building and my body have decided. It is time for me to go.

Enter summertime.

Being out of the building is the healthiest thing that could happen to me. During the summer break, my health crawls back in, tentatively at first. Then, with no mold in sight, it comes back with a vengeance. My health is literally bursting at the seams. I begin to feel as robust as I always have. My body jumps, kicks, and rejoices three days a week down the dance floor. The doctors agree for me to return to work half of the time the following school year, September 2016.

"While our bodies can reset over a long break, let's play it safe." says one of the specialists at the Occupational Health Center where I was being seen. I wanted to believe it was possible. I wanted to give it the old college try. This was my life's work we were talking about. Who was I if I wasn't a language teacher?

That summer, while my health was streaming back in, it happened.

I saw the announcement.

"Anusara Yoga Teacher Training."

Something inside soared, skipped, did cartwheels, and whispered, "Please, please, please, please, can we do this?" A yoga practitioner since 1991, I really found my practice when I discovered Anusara years later in 2000. I attribute this in large part to my teacher Pat, who gave voice to the teachings in a way that resonated with me, but also to the particular system Anusara employs.

Pat, practicing psychologist and trained Phoenix Rising Yoga coach, was in the process of becoming a certified yoga instructor with John Friend, founder of Anusara. These were the exciting start-up days of a school of Hatha yoga that would become wildly popular across the globe. Years later, its founder would fall from grace. The school would go through crisis but emerged with new wings, sustained in part by the sound teachings of Anusara's Universal Principles of Alignment.

Call it instinct. Call it intuition. Call it a desperate desire to get well. I heeded the call. That summer, when my body was re-finding normal after getting so sick, I talked to my friend Rylee, who was one of the teachers in the Anusara teacher training.

"Do you think I can do it?" I asked.

We were seated outside under a veranda at Lakhi, the yoga school where the training would be held. The sun baked the roof while we rested comfortably on the cool folding metal chairs in its shade. I gave Rylee the hard-cold facts on my health and my school year.

"Absolutely," she said. "In fact, I think it would be good for all of us to work with you through this. After all, we have students who come to the mat every day with these kinds of issues. We need to learn to be sensitive to them."

"But am I strong enough?"

I was having trouble seeing myself in any pose more strenuous than Child's pose (lying on the ground in a fetal position). Yoga all weekend long?

"You are strong enough," she said.

⅓

Anusara is a beautiful system of yoga. When I came upon it in 2000, I knew instinctively that this was the practice for me. The method is based on Five Universal Principles of Alignment that correspond to the five elements of nature. When practiced, these principles have tremendous potential to bring healing to all aspects of our lives, but particularly in our bodies.

Principle one is "Open to Grace." This is the first thing we do at the start of each new pose. We pause. We breathe. We soften our skin. We open to the greatest possibility and greatest expression of ourselves in this moment. It is a cosmic *yes*. An inhale of universal proportion. We start by aligning ourselves to our highest Self. This is the element of space. It is limitless. A great place to start when coming together with your partner.

Principle two is "Muscular Energy." This is the second action we take in our practice and in each pose. We draw energy from the earth, our foundation, toward our pelvis, hug the midline that runs up the center of our body and muscle to bone, and draw from the extremities toward the focal point of each pose. We set a boundary. We say *no*. Having a body is the first experience of no. The body is the place from which we experience our limitations. We live in it and move through space in it. It's our personal cosmic spaceship. It differentiates us from other forms. This is the element of earth. It is solid and stable. When we come together with another to find union, it's helpful to remember we are housed in different bodies. Remembering this goes a long way to bringing in curiosity. So often it is easy to get stuck in the pattern of assuming we know what the other wants or needs or believing the other will automatically intuit our own needs. Perhaps we are stuck in unconscious patterns of performance. The second principle invites us to draw into and regard ourselves with curiosity—to be open to what we find there—and to offer that same curiosity and openness to our partner.

Principle three, or "Inner Spiral," starts at the inside of the feet and spirals up the legs toward the center and around the back to the T12 vertebra at the base of the ribcage. Again and again, we draw the thighs in, back and apart. The spiral widens the back of our pelvis and roots the top of the femurs more deeply in the socket. It brings our energy into alignment again with the universal and with our own mystery. It is another cosmogonic yes. Thank goodness. It's no fun getting stuck in a no anymore than it's reasonable to be stuck forever in a yes. Since it's no fun residing indefinitely in the finiteness of our singular form, we need to connect with mystery and that which is greater than our personal selves again, and Inner Spiral takes us there. The element is water. It is receptive. It flows. It takes the shape of whatever container it finds itself in, but don't be fooled. Water is powerful.

Living in Ithaca, it is impossible not to be moved by the power of water. Cayuga Lake and the surrounding watershed is lined with gorges, deep crevasses dug over time by water always moving toward the source. Water may be soothing, but She's no fool. She will cut through whatever obstruction is in the way of her journey back home. She may do it slowly. She may even do it thoughtfully and with great tenderness, emotionality, and vulnerability, but she will certainly make her way. To bring in the third principle is to get in touch with our own sensual nature. To move into feeling, desire, want, and pleasure. To move more fully into the mystery from which we come.

Principle four is "Outer Spiral" and it moves in the opposite direction of Inner Spiral. It starts at the bottom of the back ribs and spirals downward around the backs of the thighs toward the front again and again until it comes to reside at the outside of the feet. It is a *no* current. Another boundary. What with all that water flowing, we needed a boundary. Something to contain the river so that it can flow smoothly, (even swiftly depending on the width of the river walls) and not just cover every surface of our lives. Outer spiral brings us back into the front of the body. The place where we confront life. The seat of our individuality.

"Hello world," Outer Spiral says, "I am here to greet you. To do my best to meet you as you are. To do my best to meet you as I am."

This is much easier to do now that the *shakti*, or the intelligent life force energy that runs through us as us, has a container to run through. Outer Spiral creates a new limit. The element is fire. The energy of fire moves upward, is dynamic and direct, and has the power to burn through all the *Samskaras*, or imprints left by experiences, that mark but no longer serve us. This is powerful medicine. All of it. And, it's never done. The practice of bringing in the element of fire can be helpful when we desire our partner, but old hurts that still reside in the body can arise and take us out of our experience. Fire is transformative and can help burn out or away what stands in the way of our opening.

The fifth and final principle is perhaps the most liberating of all. Principle five is "Organic Extension." Some people want to start and end here. Many of us are dominated by organic energy. We love the creative free flow movement of life and want to always reside here. We experience any kind of *no* as limiting to our innate expression, our divine wisdom, and the boundless nature of our creative spirit. Others are dominated by Muscular Energy, comforted by routine, logic, and the reliable nature of steady constructs. You can tell which sort of person you are by looking down at your feet. If your arches are high, you are ruled by Muscular Energy and could do with a bit more of Opening to Grace, Inner Spiral, and Organic Extension. If your arch is low, and you are closer to being flatfooted, you may tend to take on too much or may walk around throwing seeds and petals wherever you go, keeping little for yourself, and would most likely benefit from some of the boundaries offered by Muscular Energy and Outward Spiral.

Organic Energy radiates once the first four principles have drawn us into place. It is the final principle of alignment. We shine out our light. We extend, expand, widen, and rejoice. We share all the *shakti* we have cultivated in our practice, with the world. We make our body sing. It is beauty incarnate. It is the element of air. It is the breath. It is the movement of *prana*, the life force. It is not patterned. It is light, quick, light-hearted, creative, and always fills the space in which it moves.

It is the most delicious moment for me in each asana, where I finally can push back out toward the extremities of my body and feel the molecules of my cells moving into new territory. It is the awakening. And I love it! I could live here, I think. This is a lovely place to get to in my partnering with Chris—a free, spontaneous expression of love and desire.

While movement in and through the five principles can be somewhat linear, this is a creative process, thus, my experience can take me through them pell-mell and in no particular order. I rejoice when I have cultivated an opening that allows me to access unbridled expansiveness or union, but it's easier to get here by practicing the four other alignment principles. As much as I'd love to live here twenty-four/seven, the element of air is a pretty dry, arid place to be. Aligning to our greatest selves, means acknowledging, respecting, and cultivating all of the elements. It is a constant dance through the galaxy as we fall out of alignment and work the principles to find our way back. It is the endless pulsation of pure consciousness, and we the vehicle for consciousness to know itself. We dance and we *are* danced.

Is it any wonder that moving deeply into these practices brought my unfinished inner work to the surface? Look at what we invite in when we deeply commit to aligning ourselves to our truest nature. Everything is exposed. Everything.

Stop! My body says. This is too much.

And so, I step back. And then I step forward. A two-step gone rogue. Arms flailing. Legs kicking. Body undulating.

We dance. We dance for all we're worth; because, in fact, that is what we're dancing for. The cocreation of our lives.

ଔ

The training was a godsend. I started each weekend in tears. My return to school part time in the fall of 2016 wasn't going well. By Friday of each work week, I was half dead.

The yoga weekend trainings pushed my body's restart button. By the end of each of these weekends I was a different person. A healthy person. A happy person. A me full of potential again. Amnesia would set in. Sick me was nowhere to be found. It was as though she had never existed.

First period on Monday is sheer delight. "Reunited and it feels so good!"

I return to work aligned and renewed. Innate excitement for teaching courses through my veins. Juicy fresh delight in the sheer beauty of my students. The ability to make the subject matter sing. Oh, the joy to be again at the top of my game! I sing to myself as I move about the room as if in a dance.

Accustomed to teaching six classes a day with five different preps and rarely bringing work home at night, I have always been able to count on the force of nature that comes through in my teaching.

Halfway through second period at the start of the week, I stop dancing. I have to sit down. My students look at me bewildered.

"Can you check this for me?" asks Delphine, expecting my usual quick round of the room as I check every student's work. I pull myself up slowly from the chair, move from student to student like dried-out escargot, then spend the rest of the period teaching from a seated position. I don't recognize myself. Where did Marcy the energizer bunny go?

I make it to Friday by sheer force of will. My body has the broken record on repeat: *You can do it, Marcy. Just keep pushing, just keep moving, just keep going.* But like that record, I am broken.

Isn't this an old story?

I struggle to make it through each week until it is time for another monthly yoga teacher training weekend.

These weekends become my grounding. My salvation. With each Downward Dog, my cough progressively slows to remission. My soul reawakens—gently at first, then with more ardor, like a hungry chipmunk in winter cracking open a frozen shell to get to the soft acorn in the middle.

Then, Monday comes. Again.

ೞ

We all come to the mat as the conditioned selves we are. Our presence on the mat invites us to confront our learned nature. The nature we have acquired perhaps through many lifetimes of conditioning. This practice offers us the opportunity to greet and get to know who we are in the moment while also helping us to remember our truest nature. The pure light within. Unadulterated consciousness. Wholeness. The Self that can never be tainted, like the sun and its rays, always present, behind moving clouds.

The self I find often on the mat is the one who pushes herself mercilessly. I strive. I am impatient. I want what I want now. I compete with myself, driving my body into the final form of the pose often before it is ready.

"Open the heart," says the teacher.

I push, cajole, connive to soften that space between the shoulder blades and draw my heart toward the front of the room. I know, it's an oxymoron. How can you be softening and pushing at the same time? Just watch me.

"I thought yoga would get rid of all these tight muscles," my deep-tissue massage therapist says one day while she is working on my right shoulder.

"Yeah," I say. "But it's still me who I bring to the mat."

Coming to the mat each day allows me to bring my attention to this deep-seated tendency to push myself at all costs and set my intention to practice *maitri*, the Buddhist practice of offering loving kindness toward oneself. *Maitri* is a practice of learning, again and again, how to listen to and honor the body. How to support it to open where it has been closed, to support it to close where it has been too open. How to respect the places that are not yet ready to yield or be exposed to the light of day and coax out those that are.

As I begin to notice and tame this deeply rooted penchant to push in my personality, a space opens up. In that space, I find myself dreaming more and more of writing. The soft center of the acorn.

What if I were to call myself a writer? I wonder into that space.

I have been writing all my life. For the past fifteen years, I have written most every week, sometimes in several different writing classes. I have bought new bookcases to hold all the notebooks I filled with my thoughts and dreams.

A pastime mingling with "What if?" An index finger beckoning from the ether, "Come this way."

By the end of the first part of my yoga teacher training, the weekend just before Christmas, I find myself ready. Saying no to the bodily harm brought on each week by the moldy building allows me to claim the dormant power necessary to say yes to the burgeoning writer in me.

I am ready.

That which was set into motion the day my body whispered for me to commit myself to this yogic voyage is now rolling forward with its own momentum. It is my job to submit. To get out of my own way and respond to the call.

On our final day of the first half of the teacher training, we sit in a circle. Aria, one of our teachers, begins to pass around the talking stick, a long white delicate strand of selenite. We are invited to share whatever we want about what we have gotten out of this six-month journey. When my turn comes, my heart pumps loudly. I am sure others can see it pulsating through my shirt. I am about to announce my new intention out loud to the world. There will be no going back.

"I had no idea what I was getting into when I signed up for this training." I say. I talk about the healing that has taken place for me, this new path of yoga teaching and writing. I see it all before me, outstretched like an open hand.

Aria listens to me without showing any signs of approval or judgment, which, of course, I take as judgment. Later, she comes up to me and touches my arm gently,

"You're really going through it," she says.

Aria knows me as a French teacher. I taught her daughter Magda the previous year. Magda loved my beginner French class.

"Your class was one of the only reasons Magda wanted to stay at that school, you know," Aria says.

I didn't know. I lower my eyes. I am only beginning to sense the implications on my life of the transformation that is taking place inside of me. What *me* am I letting go to make way for the new *me*? What seeds have been planted that have not yet begun to sprout?

Chapter Four

Quest

At first, I am not sure what is happening, but soon I realize some silent part of myself is awakening through this deep dive into my yoga teacher training. I am healing. Out of this healing, a previously silent part of myself is emerging. She is saying "NO," and she is pissed.

"Can I do this?"

"Of course, you can. You are a healer."

"Can I do this?"

"*No*. Who do you think you are? Get back in your corner."

Hope and worthlessness dance wildly in me for more than a month until they spiral out of control and I hit my head—hard—just one week after the end of part one of the yoga teacher training. While preparing to leave my mother's house to return home with my family after Christmas, I give myself my fifth (and most severe) concussion.

Having had two concussions before the age of ten, one from a biking and the other from a sledding accident, the next three all happen within ten years of each other, and in the same way: I slam my head into the unforgiving steel doorframe at the top of the wheelchair ramp of our wheelchair-accessible van. The first time I do this is right after my ex-husband announces he's begun living with his girlfriend. The second time, I'm distracted, moving too fast, and not paying attention. The third time, in front of my entire family as they help us pack our van with too many gifts, the persistent onslaught of thoughts and I go down together, and stay down.

For months.

The week after my fifth concussion, the second part of my Anusara Yoga Teacher Training begins. I come into our weeklong workshop on Monday still reeling from the trauma. I spend the day lying down listening. I sit up to participate only when I can't hold myself back, which, since I love the learning, happens more frequently than it should.

On Tuesday, Demi, the third trainer, looks carefully into my face and says, "Your left pupil looks bigger than your right."

I know enough about concussions to know this is not good. At the break, she does energy work on my head. Then I try to sleep for about an hour in the main room while my peers converse loudly in the kitchen.

By the time I make it to the bathroom to have a look at my eyes, my pupils have regulated themselves. But there is a lively pressure behind my left eye that has me concerned.

Wednesday, I feel pretty normal, so I do an inversion and stand on my head.

"Are you sure that's a good idea?" Demi says.

"It will be fine," I say. It's not, of course.

I want so much to do what all the other teacher trainees are doing. So, I stand on my concussed head.

Thursday, I get craniosacral massage then go out to eat with my husband. Another big mistake. I sit in the back booth holding my head in my hands throughout the entire meal and scowl at every patron who laughs or shows other signs of enjoying their meal.

By Friday, I can barely function. I leave the immersion early Friday morning to see the doctor. I consult with Dr. Haidee, a doctor new to the family practice I've been going to for almost twenty years.

"Haidee. Is that Dutch?"

"Very good," he says approvingly.

"I'm a language teacher," I say, squinting my eyes at the bright light. He sees this and rolls his chair over to turn it off. The sound of his wheels on the industrial strength linoleum makes me wince.

After giving me a test to scale the severity of my injury he says, "You have a pretty bad concussion. You're going to be out of work for a while."

"How long?"

"At least a few weeks. Maybe a few months."

My jaw drops. I don't believe him.

Dr. Haidee orders a CAT scan to rule out any chance of a slow leak. All signs point to normal.

I stop doing yoga altogether and go to bed for two weeks straight. The crinkling of a fortune cookie wrapper is a Mac truck plowing between my ears.

By 8:00 p.m. every night for over a month, I crawl into bed, defeated. No Spanish telenovelas projected on the wall after dinner. No email. No texting. No alcohol. No getting lost in the lives of Jamie and Claire in book six of the *Outlander* series I'm reading in French. It is dinner, lights out, covers over my head, cat curled on my belly.

After two weeks of this regimen, I go back to work.

Work that was already a challenge due to my reactivity to the building becomes a nightmare. Students' voices mix like angry crows pecking at my head. No matter how many times I explain to my middle schoolers why keeping their voices down is crucial to me keeping it together, they can't do it. They nod sympathetically and maintain a respectful silence for sixteen seconds before their voices creep back to monster level.

I assign a unit of silent reading. We keep at it until the sound of soft shoes in the hallway doesn't make me rush to shut the door.

Three months later, I am mostly recovered from the concussion.

On the Saturday of our third Anusara Yoga Immersion weekend, Tina comes to talk to our group about Arjuna and the *Bhagavad Gita*. A vivid storyteller, Tina brings to life Arjuna's struggle to fulfill his destiny on the battlefield by killing half of his family. Still fragile, I lie back on my blankets to absorb her animated portrayal.

Later, we talk in the hallway. I want her to know why I wasn't sitting up to share my rapt attention while she was presenting. I tell her about my head.

"Yeah, giving a talk to yoga teachers in training is like giving a talk to kindergarteners. They're lying down or getting up or sitting on their friend's lap. You guys are being trained to do what you need to do each moment to take care of your bodies. Kindergartners and yoga teacher trainees are really quite similar," she says. I laugh, then touch my throbbing head.

Tina is an established author. Back in the fall, when my awakening was just beginning, we talked about me becoming one too. We discussed the possibility that she might help me get started.

"Do you remember the night of the Super Moon when we talked and decided we would start working together in May?"

"Yes."

"Well, the very next day my mind started spinning. All the voices that come up at the start of a new creative adventure were dogging me. I thought I might go crazy. Then I hit my head."

"Oh," she said knowingly. "You literally made yourself stop thinking."

The transformation that had begun in earnest had been knocked into a much-needed hibernation. It was showing me it had its own speed of unfoldment. The concussion was a gift. A respite. A "ready-ing." The seed that waits, seemingly dormant in the winter while it gathers up all the energy it will need to grow in the spring. Despite my best efforts, this was a process I couldn't force.

The tumultuous notion that I can shift my identity, leave behind a moldy building and a craft artfully sculpted over three decades to dedicate myself more fully to writing, healing, and yoga teaching retreats from the forefront of my mind.

However, two months later, in the middle of March 2017, I know without the shadow of a doubt I can no longer keep exposing my body to the harm mold is creating in me. I can no longer keep pushing myself to make it through to Friday. With the support of my doctors, I leave the classroom and public school teaching for good.

ଓ

I thought I had done the hard work of learning to love myself, but there is always more. Always another layer to the damn onion. When I started this training, I was not aware of the harm, subtle and less subtle that I was still perpetuating in my body. I had no way of knowing the hurricane of havoc that would come into my life by allowing so much light into the deepest recesses of my unconscious mind.

ଓ

The patterns in our lives support us. Make us feel safe. Protect us. Help us conserve our energy. Help us to get it all done. They are familiar. Like old friends you sit with comfortably on the couch. We snuggle up to our patterns. Eat popcorn, pull up the cozy fleece blanket, and sink into our patterns. Why would we want to let them go?

But some patterns, often those that reside in the deep space in our marrow, in the thick walls of our unconsciousness, in the secrets we hide even to ourselves, need to go.

I can't do this anymore. I can't keep hurting myself. As much as I love you, desire and recognize the importance of this union, I can't keep pushing myself physically in bed, I say to myself before I figure out how to say it, and mean it, to Chris.

Time and again I am brought into touch with my tendency to push the boisterous *I can do that!*, that grew as a shield of protection behind which something tender could stay hidden. I begin to see the parallels of "Make it to Friday," "Go deeper into the pose!" and "Let's go straight toward orgasm!" while a quieter voice is saying, "No. Stop. This isn't working."

What is less apparent to me yet is the quiet *yes* that often never gets to surface.

The quiet *no* and the quiet *yes* are both sacred. Both demand deep respect, but they ask for something distinct. The first asks to *stop pushing* already and *start listening*. The second asks for a nudge, a gentle push, an invitation to move toward our potential.

The body has its own wisdom. At first, it speaks so softly as to be easily missed. The regular practice of yoga helps bring this more subtle voice into my awareness. I stumble. I step over, bulldoze through, or ignore the quieter voices there—so deep are these ingrained patterns.

But I am learning to be patient with myself and the process. I am learning to move closer and closer to honoring a deeper expression of myself. I bring this evolving practice into my yoga classes and my private practice, invite my yoga students and my clients into this dance of attention to the subtler, softer voices that hold deeper truths.

CB

We have seen what we are capable of. We have gotten a glimpse, maybe even spent some time in the expansiveness of our own beauty. Then we go back home to the deep divot in the couch. The blanket has become scratchy or leaves a rash on our skin. The popcorn gets stuck in our throat and causes us to cough for an hour before bed. Something is no longer working. But what? Our patterned existence has gotten just a wee bit too small for us. Like a hermit crab, we need to shed our confining shell in search of one that can house this larger self. One that's large enough to grow into.

This is what I came home to find. Straight off the plane from Mexico and into bed, I find it. This sacred *no* came up like a giant tiger in the weeds, coiled, ready to pounce on its prey.

"We have to do this differently," I say the next day seated across from Chris on my yoga mat. "We have been doing it your way for the last fifteen years. How about we try doing it mine?"

The truth is that Chris has always been an attentive lover, ready and willing to do whatever it was that I wanted or needed. Generous to a fault, our lovemaking has always put my needs first. It's just that I don't always really know what my needs are. I am so conditioned toward *pleasing my partner, saying yes before I'm ready,* and to *things looking a certain way*, that I don't always know how to truly honor myself. I don't always slow things down to hear the quieter voice ready and waiting to guide me.

I bring my yoga practice to bed.

"Let's just breathe together," I say.

We have often started our lovemaking ritual this way, tuning in to our breath. Sitting. Bringing our attention to the present moment. But the stakes have changed. There is a new intention. A deeper commitment to our lovemaking being a spiritual practice. A practice of deep listening.

"I'm bored with purely physical pleasure," I say. "Sometimes it's just what I want, don't get me wrong. But, we are so much more than our bodies."

We are mystery.

While we have experienced the transcendental in sex, have had the heart-opening, soul-melting unions that stir my loins again later in the day when I think back on our lovemaking, these sorts of comings together have become more rare, and the *give each other physical pleasure and then go on with the day*, more the norm.

"This is just what happens to couples who have been together for a long time," says Chris.

"I want more." I say.

I want more. I don't care how long we've been a couple; I want more.

☃

For years, in order to achieve orgasm, I have been creating fantasies in my head. The issue for me is that many of my fantasies stem from the abuse that was done so early to my body. Like the main character in *Belle de Jour*, that which is erotic as adults is often linked to our senses being stirred in early-life experience.

For a long time, I felt bad about the fantasies that would form in my mind during sex. I was ashamed. I kept them to myself. Then, I tried a new tact. Why should I be ashamed? Wasn't this giving power to my oppressor yet again? Why should I feel bad about what seemed to come naturally to me? Even if the fantasies often evoked a feeling of a boundary not being respected, weren't they mine, thus okay? The short answer is yes. The long answer is *I want more.*

I share my *"jardin* secret," with Chris. We talk about it. Turn it over in our minds and our hearts.

"Did you have to have a fantasy this time?" he asks as we snuggle after making love.

Most times, the answer is yes. The fantasies vary. Some are the classic babysitter or older male who takes pleasure from a young female. Another favorite? Adult man jerks off inappropriately in front of a young girl. Is it any wonder these images come back to haunt me and in my most intimate inner space?

For so many years, I was willing to pay this price for the opening that would occur afterward. The closeness. The ease. The way my body had moved into *yes*. The juicy quality I felt linger in my loins. The touches before and after in the kitchen as we prepared food. The prolonged kisses where our two essences would meld and flow into something greater.

It was worth it. Until it wasn't.

ভ

"I need something different. I can't do this anymore. I can't push myself to be sexual so that we can feel close. I can no longer hold orgasm or consummation as the ultimate goal. It is too limiting. Too small." My voice trails off as my eyes focus on the long line of ants walking up the wall toward the skylight. I'm back in Joel's upstairs office for a therapy session.

"You need to strengthen your *hara*," Joel says. "The hara resides just below the belly. It is the seat of differentiation. You need to make yours stronger."

I am seated across from Joel in a cross-legged position. The chair is large, the cushion under me soft and supple. I pick at my toenails as my eyes now alternate between the long line of ants and the tall plants growing up into the two dormer windows on the ceiling behind him.

"Why do you do it?" he asks.

"What? Orgasm at all costs?"

Joel just looks at me.

"For completion, I guess."

I don't know how to tell him that our regular practice of lovemaking has been essential to keeping our couple strong and healthy. How knowing we would consummate our union every week regardless of what was going on or who was in the house or whether or not I felt like it to begin with, pushed me to move through my thick resistance, get to the other side of mistrust to see, feel, and believe the love and the beauty in the eyes of my husband. How Chris's ardent desire for me was the push I needed to keep coming together. How my ardent desire for the freedom that resided just on the other side of orgasm pushed me through all the monsters that showed up every week to keep us apart.

"He didn't do this to me," I say. "He is not the author of why it is so hard for me to open up to love."

"What do you want?" he asks.

"I want it to be easier," I say.

"What's behind that?"

I start to cry.

"It's so old," I inhale through the tears streaming down my face. "I just want to be seen. To be known deeply."

"Yes," he nods.

And I know I'm on the right track.

○3

In bed with my husband, I start by tuning in. I listen for the quieter voice. I slow things down. I attempt to notice when I'm pushing myself and pause. I take a moment to be curious about what my body is telling me. It helps to start by making space for the *no*, a *no* I've been so conditioned as a woman to ignore, before I move toward *yes*.

My partner joins me in this journey. Mostly, he is willing to slow down, follow my rhythm, though he can grow impatient when our time together is limited. But, while he is willing to slow down, he has never been able to *guide* me. This, I am learning, is *my* job. It pisses me off. How much easier it would be if my partner could just intuit what is true for me every moment; feel what my body wants before I even know myself! How much easier to have a partner who could show me the way.

I make mistake after mistake, remind myself to move with a light touch. Remind myself that this is a dance. That it's not about getting it right, but about inviting the novel as my cells cry for something deeper, more authentic.

"I hear you," I say, like the dutiful parent I never felt I had growing up. "And I am doing my very best to honor you."

Chapter Five

Mother

"You have a complicated relationship with your mother," Chris says. *No shit*, I think.

I hate him for saying it.

"All children have complicated relationships with their parents," I say.

My mother and I have come a long way—a way paved by each of us doing our own work—healing work that ultimately lead her to become a clinical social worker and me to become a healer. It's taken us a long time to get here. We can usually make our way through struggles and bumps in the road nowadays without all hell breaking loose. And while I can still feel overwhelmed by my mother—I mean *she is still* my mother—I have grown to count on her to be there when I need her, to pull herself back, or reign in her demons when I just need her to listen.

Last weekend was an exception.

Mother's Day.

I can scarcely recall a childhood birthday, major holiday, or even a cross-country meet I was running in that didn't end in a fight with my mother. It was almost a given. Such days caused our deepest dynamics to surface—my desperate need for intuitive, attentive mothering coupled with my immediate cellular rejection of anything she might try to offer and her urgent desire to connect without knowing how to reach me. A setup that could trigger her darkest side.

The year I turned eleven, my mother bought me a skirt and a blouse from J. C. Penny for my birthday. The top was fuchsia, and the skirt was pleated and gray with a subtle fuchsia stripe running through the fabric. The package was wrapped with care and tied with a bow. I tried them on and didn't like them. It just wasn't the right style for me at that time. I knew I was taking a risk by being honest when my mother asked how I liked it.

"It's okay. You can tell me," she said.

I took a deep breath. "I don't think it's really me."

We were standing in the old farm kitchen at the back of the third house we'd lived in since she divorced my father. Tension ignited the air. In a flash, my mother flew into a rage. Frothing at the mouth, she left the room wringing her hands before she came back to strike the stinging psychic blow.

"You don't appreciate anything I do. You ungrateful little shit!"

She then grabbed the object closest to her and hurled it across the room. She might have hit my sister or the dog on her way out just to relieve some more of her own pain. It took her hours to calm herself down. *What hurt had my rejection of her gift triggered?*

My mother could lose control, and often did, even as she worked in therapy to integrate and master this rage. She started therapy when I was five and continued pretty much until her therapist died of cancer just a few years ago. Her road to healing has been rutted and long, and while there were casualties along the way, there were also intermittent rays of sunshine.

To my sister and me growing up, it wasn't always clear what would bring such fits of blind madness to the surface, though sometimes, later in our teens, we could see her teetering on the edge, and gave her just the push that would take her over.

Ours was a house of broken mirrors. The reflections of ourselves we saw fractured our spirits and left our fragile egos in pieces.

I had forgotten what this rage looked like, except that some of it lives on in me. There are times today when that place gets triggered and it takes everything I have not to strike out.

My mother's father was a WWII vet. A complicated, brilliant man, with a PhD in psychology specializing in color perception, my grandfather went on to work for Kodak and terrorize his family. My mother tells stories of him holding a gun to her and her siblings' heads at the dinner table when he was drunk. The war raged inside him, and he brought it to dinner. Just as when my own father's post-traumatic stress was at its height, back then there was no word, no diagnosis, for the haunting after-effects of war on the mind and body. My grandfather lived his nightmares drunk and shared them with the whole family.

Drawn to the vibrant flamboyance of his daughter, the way her personality could fill the room, her flare for the dramatic, her skill at dance, piano, and voice, he visited my mother's bedroom at night. She was his charm, and he put her on his necklace and wore her under his shirt. What a colossal confusing mess for a smart young girl desperate for the love and attention of an ingenious, yet troubled father.

Perhaps by instinct, perhaps sensing the intimacy that had developed between her husband and her oldest child, my grandmother was ruthless with my mother. She froze her out. Endlessly critical of her talents, she broke her down every chance she got. Nothing my mother ever did was good enough in her belittling, jealous eyes, while she showered her second child with often unmerited praise and affection.

The injustice. The sheer violence and destructiveness. It is a marvel that anyone with such a story could survive, much less find her way in life.

How much of my mother's traumatic experience lives on in me?

The field of epigenetics shows that trauma can live in the cellular memory of animals for many generations. A study on a self-effulgent

55

water worm, reviewed by Sciencedaily.com in April 2017, shows that environmental factors can cause genetic expression to change and remain changed for as many as fourteen generations. In the August 21, 2015 publication of *The Guardian*, an article entitled "Study of Holocaust Survivors Finds Trauma Passed on to Children's Genes" posits that children whose parents were interned in a concentration camp, experienced torture, or had to hide to survive, had a genetic change that made them more likely to develop stress disorders than Jewish children whose parents did not have those traumatic experiences.

We carry the evidence of the stories our forebears have lived in our bodies.

I came into this world carrying the genetic deviations caused by incest and childhood sexual abuse. *Was I destined from the start to live my own tale of violation, abuse, and neglect simply by being my mother's daughter?*

The week preceding Mother's Day was a difficult one for me emotionally. The weight of my identity transition weighed heavily on my heart. Grappling with the notion of being a sick person, unable to see my future, I was struggling with the loss of my teaching profession. I arrived at my mother's house feeling vulnerable and that vulnerability made me tense. I resolved not to share any of this on Mother's Day. I wrapped myself inside the silken walls of a cocoon.

Then I had a scotch.

I could no longer hold onto my defenses. The chrysalis dissolved. I wanted to talk. Share how I was doing. But the pace of the conversation at the table was too fast.

After I announced I wanted to share something, my stepsister, Elsa, stood over me with her hands on her hips saying, "Well go on. Tell us!" As I told my story, everyone at the table became furious. Furious at the school district. Furious at my principal. Furious at Donald Trump for creating an atmosphere of "Fuck You!" to anyone who needed extra support.

I was overwhelmed by the fury in the room.

Then the solutions started coming at me.

"You could come and work in my school district," Elsa offered.

"Couldn't you take on private students?" ventured Martin, Elsa's father, my mother's third husband, and my stepfather for over twenty-five years.

"That is just outrageous!" my mother, sitting to my right, yelled loudly into my ear.

I knew people were trying to be supportive, but I needed it all to stop. The horses were running wild. I tried to bring them back into the stable.

"I appreciate your indignation and all the solutions you are offering, but that's not really helpful to me right now," I said.

All discussion stopped. Elsa went off to the bathroom. Martin started clearing the table. Chris did the dishes in the kitchen. But my mother stayed. She turned toward me, still ready to pounce on my adversaries.

Her intensity was punching holes in my fragile skin. I tried to redirect her fearsome energy. I asked for something softer—a quieter, gentler place. My request was the shrill note that breaks the crystal. I don't know what I said, but to my mother, it was yet another rejection. She turned the rage she had been feeling at the injustice of my situation on me and erupted.

Soon she was coming at me, like when I was a child, her body taut like a rubber band ready to snap.

"I'm done talking about it," I said trying to make it stop.

"Now you're just trying to hurt me," her eyes darted wildly from me to Martin.

"She just doesn't want to talk about it anymore. She's done," Martin said from the kitchen.

I was still seated in my chair. My mother was up pacing like a wild panther. I sensed imminent danger. How had this gone so wrong so quickly?

I probably shouldn't have had that whiskey, I thought to myself.

"Stop Mom." I said, "Just stop." She came at me again.

"*I* wasn't the one trying to solve your problem. That wasn't me." She shouted as she looked straight at Elsa then at Martin.

I felt embarrassed. I wanted to protect Elsa from my mother as much as I wanted to protect myself.

"Stop saying that," I insisted.

She continued. I watched as her flame got brighter and brighter.

Elsa sat down across from me at the table as though the house wasn't about to go up in smoke. She put out her hands. I put mine in hers. My mother was now in the kitchen ranting behind my back. I pretended not to hear.

"I'm forty-eight years old. Can you believe I have to reinvent myself?" I said to Elsa's now receptive face.

"It happens," she said simply.

My mother came and sat down next to me again. Instinctively, I leaned away from her.

"Why are you leaning away from me?" she asked.

"Because you're scaring me."

"That's ridiculous." Again, she came at me with angry words. What transpired next is blurry at this point, but somehow, we had gotten out of our chairs and were standing in the kitchen.

"All you do is criticize me," she yelled.

"Bullshit," I said.

She kept coming at me, venom on her tongue. I kept asking her to stop. She wouldn't. She couldn't. And then it came. The explosion lit up her body and shot out of her eyes as her hand moved to hit me. She stopped it. Barely. But not before I saw it. I grabbed my things and walked toward the door.

"Happy Fucking Mother's Day," I said as I walked out. I could still hear her yelling about what a brat I was loudly in the kitchen to whoever would listen.

I waited in the car. Watched as Elsa and Martin made their way out to Elsa's car, Chris not far behind. They talked for a few moments, then Chris came over and got into the driver's seat.

The ride home was long and silent. I kept replaying the fight in my head, grateful I was no longer the dependent, vulnerable child who couldn't get away.

"What did you and Elsa and Martin talk about next to the car?" I asked forty-five minutes into the trip.

"Martin told a story about how when he was eight, he was at some conference with a friend and his friend's mother. In the middle of the conference his friend's mother started having a nervous breakdown. All he wanted was to get out of there and hide outside."

The next day, I told a writer friend of mine what had happened on Mother's Day.

Just as our cells amass the stories of generations, my excavation of the past roared into the here and now.

"The writing is working on you," she said.

CS

Everything hurts today. My body aches as though I am getting the flu. My head feels heavy. My sinuses sting. My heart, well, it seems to want to speak or, rather, moan long and loud. There is a primitive element to it. A long-ago knowing. I have summoned it here. But am I ready? Do I know how to hold myself as the ancient pain, the ancient rage emerges?

Yesterday, a writing day, was what I would call a "big" day. As I commit more and more to the exploration of sexual abuse and make my own experience the subject, the content of my days begins to align with this purpose. I wanted to bring my new "knowing" to the page. But what had I learned? What had I felt? What had I seen? Did I want to summon it again to get it down on the page?

At my weekly writing circle, for the first time in all my years of writing and sharing my words publicly, I touched on the subject of sexual abuse. I was careful and didn't go so far as to share any intimate details of what had been done to me. I wrote of something much safer. I wrote about what had been done to my mother, and thus, by default, to me:

> *When I was eleven, I started keeping a journal. It was small, with a red cover and blank pages. It had a small golden clasp with a lock.*
>
> *I recall the sweet sensation of letting my deepest thoughts scroll out onto the page. This, followed by a crippling fear. What if my mother ever found out?*
>
> *Her presence loomed large, like a huge gray cumulus threatening rain. Somehow, I thought, even with this tiny golden lock, she would know what I was writing. There was no true privacy anywhere in my life— not in my mind, not in my body.*
>
> *I censored myself. Held back from telling the truth. Instinctively, I knew this journaling had potential, but my truest thoughts weren't safe. Anywhere.*
>
> *When I opened one of the drawers to the white chipped desk in my bedroom, I found my mother's diaphragm.*

Is it a hat for a small cat? *I wondered.* What is this plastic house it lives in? *I touched it, felt it's soft latex center and hard outer rib. It sat in the drawer where I had chosen to keep my diary. A haunting symbol whose meaning only comes clear as I write this. Just as my mother's diaphragm had no business being in my desk, her father and his groping hands had no business coming into her room at night.*

No, I could not write in this journal, a gift from my mother who knew I had secrets to reveal to myself, who sensed the heavy weight of history—hers and mine—that I carried, boundaryless, through the gardens and the fields and in every walk of life.

This short essay was followed by another perhaps more indicative of my struggle to enter the waters I needed to penetrate, to know this part of myself.

We were invited to choose a print of a painting done by a local visual artist, Beatrice. Beatrice's work is largely abstract. She uses paint to create a visual landscape, a mix of blots, subtle colors, black lines, and bright spaces. One of the writers in our group found her work offensive, "If it were on the wall at the diner, it might cause me to regurgitate." I don't share this view. Like most well-done abstract work, I find that if I spend some time with it, I usually begin to see myself. In the piece I chose, there was one part that grabbed my attention:

There are stories to be told. Our stories. Lives of truths and lies, knotted and gnarly—waiting to be carefully, lovingly unwound.

Tread lightly, they say, yours is a sacred art. A Yeoman's task, and to do it justice requires great care and kindness. A gentle touch but a fearless probe into the depths of memory and sensation.

Hold on, dear peaceful warrior, it will be a bumpy, often chaotic, but ultimately rewarding ride. Buckle up if you wish, but keep the clasp at hand, for you may need to rip it off to dance in the sudden rush of lilies or unsuspected breeze that touches your temples, dries wet tears, and moves wisps of hair from your eyes.

The buckle is there to protect, not to confine. You are in charge of the buckle. Like Bacchus guards the door of drunkenness and surrender.

The underworld awaits. Dead heads float in the sea of Hades; rotting hands reach up and grab at your leg. Eyes, putrid, spin in morbid orbits. But that deadly sea is also your salvation. Dip your toe in, and then a foot. It will not kill you. It will release you. Someday, maybe, you may learn to swim freely among the corpses, familiar with their scent. Today, a toe, a finger that lingers at the surface of tumultuous waters. Then write. Give it everything you have. There are stories that want to be told and they are circling your head.

As my turn to read approached, my heart began to beat more quickly. I considered passing, keeping my thoughts and words to myself, and then it was my turn. And I read, knowing that the power of secrets to possess us lessens as we begin to share them. The power of my mother's story over me and every aspect of my life was loosening its grasp. The power of my own deep wounds of violation, from faces I don't recall and faces that populated my days, was slowly, maybe even surely, unfastening its clutch on my roots. I had put my big toe into those waters and brought it back out, still intact.

C8

"If you were to write what you couldn't, didn't dare to write back then . . . how old were you?"

"Ten or eleven."

"If what you wrote was locked up in a vault, impenetrable, even from your sense that your mother could know it without even reading it, what would you have written?"

I am sitting across from Joel. We have adjusted our comfy chairs to face each other in perfect alignment. I blink my eyes, study the line of ants walking up the opposite wall to the left of the Chinese painting of a tiger. It is hot. Summer has erupted for two days, in the middle of the third week of May. The air is heavy. My chest heaves as I take a deep breath.

"I hate you."

Joel's gaze is intense.

"Yes." he says.

I sit with this for a moment, feel it out. See how and where it resides in me.

"This is power," he says. "It is good that you are wearing a black t-shirt today."

"Why?"

"Black is the color of power."

"Why is it okay to say that I hate my mother?"

"Because it's true."

For some reason this strikes me as funny. I start to laugh, then can't stop. We laugh together. Why is it funny that it's true that I hate my mother? *Does the idea of hating my mother now seem preposterous to me? There were certainly times when I hated her back then, but now?*

I tell the story of how, when my father was first hospitalized for manic depression, he dreamed he killed his father. I was nineteen, visiting him in the psych ward after his first long manic-psychotic rampage.

"I thought that was a good sign," I said, "that he dreamed he killed his father." After all, what was he really killing? The abuser? The abuse? The injustice? The part of himself that kept him from living fully.

"Is your mother still alive?"

"Yes. She lives about an hour or so away. I saw her last weekend, and we got in a colossal fight. On Mother's Day."

He nods as though this was to be expected.

"When I first started therapy, I was in my early twenties, I would talk about my mother all the time. Everything I said had to do with her, how she felt, what was going on for her. Finally, my therapist said, 'Do you realize you're only talking about your mother? That you're not talking about yourself?' I didn't. I didn't have a clue that my mother's psyche took up so much space, leaving me absent to my own experience or ability to know myself. There were so few boundaries."

Joel brings me back to the present. He asks me to feel the chair beneath me. The armrests supporting my arms.

"Now feel the energy moving from your belly up to your heart."

"Just beyond the old hate is the feeling of invisibility," I say.

"Existential annihilation."

I close my eyes to tune in. I can feel it, this age-old place. So familiar. When the room spins with quiet, Joel chimes in again.

"What you are doing is alchemical. You're turning stone to gold. Or coal into a diamond. Or sand into a pearl. It can't be done without immense pressure or immense patience. This has always been the path."

❦

At the start of our next session, I motion with my hands around my lower extremities. "I have never felt safe. I have always felt somehow that my body didn't belong to me. That it wasn't my own. There was no safe place growing up. I can still feel that way. I felt that this morning with my husband."

"How so?"

"Just lying in bed. Like I couldn't control what was coming in, what was about to happen to me. That I couldn't stop it." I recall the trees walking toward my window at night. The abject terror. Nowhere to hide. The certainty that I would die that night. Be engulfed. Suffocated. Taken over.

"But I feel safe here," I say.

"Good," Joel says, "I am honored."

I go on to tell Joel how my workers' comp lawyer seems to have taken a shine to me.

"'Marcy,' my lawyer said to me on our last phone call after asking me to get together for a drink, 'I'm 100 percent behind you. More than that. 200 percent. You have no idea. I have developed personal feelings for you. I think of you every day. I've wanted to call you every day.'"

Joel listens as I recount this conversation.

"Can you believe this? It's happening again," I say, eyes opened, wide and wild. My lawyer is turning seventy soon. He has asked me to go out to hear music at night, which I declined. He said he thought we'd make great dance partners.

"I don't know," ventures Joel. "Maybe he lives in poverty. Perhaps he sees something very alive in you that he wants for himself. Maybe it's innocent. Maybe it's not. But you can probably deal with him nicely, not bonk him over the head with it. The more your boundaries are clear, the less he'll have to grab onto."

"I really need him to be my lawyer," I say.

"So, keep that clear."

Joel looks at me. We are almost out of time.

"Stand up," he says. I stand. He shows me how to place my feet. He raises his right hand, I raise mine. Our palms meet.

"Now say, 'This is mine,' as you push against my hand and step your back foot forward."

I do as he says. We play with this for about two minutes. His pressure on my hand gets stronger and stronger. I push back, find the voice that comes from my belly. I push him away, again and again as I repeat, "This is mine."

"So, you DO like older men," my lawyer says the next time I see him as I take the last bite of my sandwich. We are sitting at an outdoor cafe sharing lunch on a sunny day. I have just told him my husband is sixty years old.

"I like my husband," I reply, to be clear.

On our walk back to his office and my parked car, he turns and says, "So, will you dance with me? Your husband would probably be jealous."

"I would have to bring him along," I say, once again, to be clear. *And this is mine,* I think to myself as I get in my car.

C&#x8;

My mother's fingers are knotted and bent with age. She is seventy-four at the time I write this, though most people think she is much younger. She takes pride in her youthful look, in the sound way her body moves, its supple flexibility, its well-preserved shape. But her fingers, those final knuckles just below the nail beds, they tell the story of a long fight. So many battles lost. So many won. And still a few ahead.

My mother's fingers and hands bathed and swaddled and held me as an infant, brushed my hair, and helped me dress as a child. They boiled and served too many frozen green peas. Poured glasses of milk that would never be drunk. Mashed banana into the French Toast egg batter so that we would get one more fruit a day in our childhood diet.

Later, but not much later, those same hands struck out in fits of rage gone amuck. They struck my sister's growing body, again and again, leaving bruises that would never fade. They slammed doors. Shook windows. Hit the dog. Grabbed for knives. Instilled a fear that took root and grew into an enormous evergreen, creating everlasting doleful shade.

Those hands, that I now find exquisite in their crooked shape, try as they did, never managed to comfort me as a child. I learned to distrust those hands and, with that, missed out on the warmth they may have offered. Sometimes, even today, when those hands touch me, I feel them searching for something I don't want to give. They step right over the boundary of my skin, and reach in too far, exceeding their rightly grasp. They can feel like the hands of a lover, seeking to penetrate my body and my soul. Looking to unite. To become one.

They say too much. They tell too much. They want too much.

When this happens, I want them off me. Back, to the boundary they never thought to look or listen for. I want them to wait for my sign. The green light that says it is okay to enter. That says I am yours to touch. Even if that day may never come. So, when my mother touches me, and my skin bristles, I gently let go of her hand or move myself just beyond her reach. Back to safety. Back to myself.

αβ

Even though moms often get a bad rap, there is really no way to do healing work and not look at the mother-daughter relationship.

Yesterday, in my session with Joel, I talk about her again.

"She really showed up for me when I called yesterday."

He smiles, eyes bright.

"She listened?"

"She did. I had to raise my voice once to get her to hear me, which I'm not sure she noticed since she was still talking, but yes. She listened. Took me in. I got to cry and go deep into my grief, sadness, and guilt."

"Guilt?"

"Yes. I took away Zain's ability to get relief from sitting when I took out the Endless Pool in our house. I can't help but wonder if any of this would be happening if he were still able to swim regularly like he used to."

In the midst of my mold-induced health crisis, I became highly sensitized to the chlorine gas emitted by the Endless Pool in the addition at the back of the house. This room communicated directly with Zain's bedroom, and those tiny particles of chlorine found their way in. As utterly despondent as it made me feel to do so, we had to remove the pool, or remove me from the house. Since Zain had moved out, we chose the pool.

Now, a year after moving out, Zain has developed an open sore that won't heal above his rectum, presumably from spending all night on that spot sleeping on his back and sitting all day long in his wheelchair.

"Oh. Yes. I remember."

On the phone, my mother reminds me that Zain's neuromuscular specialists at Strong Memorial Hospital in Rochester approved the removal of the pool. Dr. C wrote at the time when we were wrestling with the decision:

> "Marcy you need to do what's best for your health. And, most importantly, you have no reason to feel guilty about this in any way: you have done an amazing job all along with Zain and he knows it. Zain will be able to arrange alternate ways of swimming if he decides to. Perhaps once a week or whenever he can do it will be sufficient."

Since Zain's birth, my mother has been 100 percent at my side. She's been 120 percent at my side as I deal with Zain's diagnosis and subsequent care needs. I say so to Joel.

"I think she would have loved to have been able to show up that way for us when we were growing up, but she wasn't there yet."

"I would hate to be held accountable for twenty-five-year-old me," he says. Then he quotes someone who said, "We were all cannibals once."

I haven't seen my mother since the blow-up at her house a few weeks back where I got to see the demons that while mostly dormant, can still be stirred from her depths; the same demons that terrorized her youth and then my sister's and mine.

My mother has been able to show up so differently over the past twenty years of Zain's (and my) life because of her own deep commitment to healing. She never gave up on herself, even in her worst moments. She kept coming back to the table, loving us fiercely even while her demons lurched forth, unbidden, causing chaos and harm. She kept at the business of healing her wounds, even those that would never fully be healed, and slowly grew into a more emotionally stable and reliable mother (and very stable and reliable grandmother).

This morning, lying in bed as Chris pulls up the shades, revealing another blue-sky day, I think about my complicated relationship with my mother. The way that I can still feel lost in her presence, the way she can fill the space with her flamboyant, dramatic personality, asking for the attention of all in the room. The very largeness of her as I struggle to be separate, take up space, even shine.

While this is not always the dynamic, it often still is and she and her husband, affectionately known as Dappy by his grandkids, will be visiting us this Sunday. *How can I prepare myself,* I wonder, *so that I don't shrink, get lost, angry, and resentful?*

When I can see the child in my mother still needy for attention, a person struggling to come fully into the world like me, a softness touches my heart, and I know I have found a key.

In *Falling on a Soft Mat*, Hafiz writes:

". . . A young child first learning to walk and very likely to fall may be allowed to do so by a wise guardian or teacher if there is a soft mat beneath his body that will cushion it from harm.
There is a soft rug you can place around others, it is forgiveness, it is charity.
We are all still learning to walk—and fly—in ways; kin help each other."

Perhaps we are all still just learning to walk—and fly—as Hafiz suggests, but that we can help soften each other's journey by understanding this.

Even our mother's.

Especially our mother's.

Chapter Six

Little Me

Chris and I are taking one of our afternoon walks in the woods that join our land. We have just crossed the Coy Glen stream heading back toward home. I am on the lookout for red newts, but it is dry out today and they are probably staying moist under a rock in the streambed.

"Here. A perfect acorn just for you," Chris says as he stands up and plops an acorn into my hand.

I love acorns. The smooth bottom and impeccable marbled brown French beret each one wears on the top. I turn this one over in my hand and notice a hole just below the bottom ridge of its hat.

"It's not perfect. It has a hole in it," I say.

"That's Nature for ya."

We walk along, stepping over roots jutting up in the well-worn path and I ponder Chris's words, so full of simple wisdom and truth.

That *is* Nature. Riddled with imperfections, exceptions, what we might even see as deformities or aberrations. All part of her plan. All just a natural part of life.

I can't help wondering, if this acorn were to grow into a tree, would this mark in the original seed show up in its mature form? Would the tree, as it grows, hold the memory of something missing or would it be able to compensate, little by little, as it grew? Would this hole cause it to grow a lump at the base of its trunk, have slightly disfigured bark, or would it still be able to grow tall and straight?

I notice how few trees stand without some sort of visible imperfection. The forest is filled with trees possessing every sort of oddity you can imagine. The tree that grows straight upward with unmarred bark and branches filled evenly with leaves is hard to come by and far from the norm.

Where did we get the idea that our lives or our bodies would grow to full form without all kinds of marks, strange growths, broken bark, and branches that never bear fruit? From where does this unattainable standard of perfection as norm come? What not-so-subtle form of aggression has indoctrinated us? We are relentless with ourselves when we don't, when we can't, measure up. Who, on a walk through the forest, would look upon nature's imperfections (if they even were to see them as such) and think, *The forest must be wrong?* Why, then, do we do this so ruthlessly to ourselves?

Last summer I learned the story of the twin acorns, one gone to seed in the center of a lush pasture, with nutrient rich soil, plenty of space to grow, and all-day sunlight. The other, to find its place in the craggy slope of an unforgiving rocky mountain pass. The first grows to be enormous with nothing to slow the spread of its branches or the yearly rings that make its trunk massive and strong. The second has to fight for footing, push up against unforgiving winds that cause its bark to swirl, never to grow to full height. The first may live to be 400 years old. All those who see it marvel at its luminosity and grandeur. The second may live to be forty-two, if it's lucky, but the struggle against the elements has made it exquisite, original, unique. An experienced woodworker would know how to showcase its unusual patterns and sell anything made of it at top dollar. Having fought for every centimeter of its life, each inch of growth is filled with extraordinary character and presence.

No passerby can set her gaze upon either tree and not be humbled by its glory.

Each started with an acorn. Each had two very different experiences and created two equally majestic trees.

But when the wind dies down, does the tree on the craggy slope know it can rest? That it can let go and soften into the warm rays of the sun? When a great storm comes, does the great oak in the clearing know how to stand its ground? Has it learned to withstand the harshest elements of life?

ᦗ

A writing friend suggests I try telling my story from the perspective of the child who has lived it. Only I have no idea how to do that. That very same week, I notice the workshop "Healing the Inner Child and Shamanic Journeying," chalked on the board at Lakhi.

Pioneered in 1990 by John Bradshaw in his groundbreaking work, *Homecoming: Reclaiming and Championing Your Inner Child*, the idea of healing your inner child has now become cliché. The expression "Inner Child," tends to elicit all kinds of judgment in people, including me! However, the timely appearance of this offering feels like a sign. I open myself to the possibility that this workshop might just give me something I need.

ᦗ

I turn into the parking lot. The car in front of me also turns in. It is a Ford Bronco, and it's left turn signal blinks slowly. Surely.

The entrance to the yoga studio parking lot is rutted and full of potholes. I do my best to keep my tires on the high ground, but it is impossible. The front-end dips and heaves and then is back again. I park along the front, leaving ample space between my car and the next. Somehow, leaving ample space seems appropriate today. Even without knowing it, I have begun to draw my boundaries.

I count the cars. There are seven so far. The workshop, I am told, will be small. Doing this sort of work requires a safe container. Intimacy.

Intimacy and the trust of perfect strangers. Except not everyone in the room is a perfect stranger.

I walk into the kitchen area, the first part of the long corridor that leads to the downstairs bathroom. As I pour hot water over my teabag, Susan, a woman I haven't seen in ten years walks into the kitchen.

"You," I say.

"I know," she replies.

Jasmina, one of the leaders of the "Healing the Inner Child and Shamanic Journeying," workshop, stands within earshot.

Susan is wearing bright colors, as usual. Her pants are crimson orange and her sweater is rose pink. Her breathing seems shallow as though she is weighing a heavy dilemma.

"Is this okay?" I ask.

"I don't know," she says.

"I could leave," I offer.

Susan turns to Jasmina and says, "I used to be her therapist." Her voice seems strained.

"I always feel like the people who show up are the ones who are meant to be here," Jasmina says.

"I need to go outside and contemplate this," Susan replies, making no eye contact with me. She stopped making eye contact with me the moment I offered to leave.

Susan leaves in a flurry, leaving me and Jasmina alone with each other and our tea.

"It's okay with me if we're both here," I offer. I check in with my body to make sure it agrees with me. I acknowledge that I might not even know if this is okay yet, but for the moment, my body is quiet. I have paid my $70.00 and prepared myself for the unknown of the next three hours. I'm ready to go in, or so I think.

Soon, Jasmina leaves and goes outside. On her way she motions me into the yoga room where the ceremony will be held. I decline. I don't want to go in until I know if I will be staying. I sit on the bench in the corner of the kitchen area and wait. I sip my tea. I have chosen a Tulsi tea bag for kidney and liver detox. It tastes disgusting. I get up and dump it out. I choose another Tulsi tea bag with rose and lavender and pour myself a new cup. I let the steam rise up into my nostrils as it steeps.

A few minutes later, I hear feet on the wooden floor. I stand and greet Susan's flushed face. While they were gone, I started getting a pretty clear "no," message from my body, but then she says, "It's okay. I guess we're doing this."

Jasmina, who is walking behind Susan, gives me a gentle smile and nods. We go in.

The room has already been set up. I take my seat on a blanket to the left of Aria. Susan sits to her right. They are close friends.

I roll up a blanket and sit. Aurora, the other workshop leader, sits holding a hand drum at the far end of the room in front of the Ganesh statue and altar. She seems frail, like a small bird. Her voice is soft and lilting. She offers herself as a question, as though ready to be rejected. Something inside of me *is* rejecting her, I notice, and I ask it to give her a chance.

In the middle of the room there is a circle of feathers, crystals, and recently cut flowers. Jasmina invites us to take anything that speaks to us to hold during the ceremony. One of the crystals, a dark, dense fragment with a soft buffed-looking top, speaks to me, but I don't respond. I don't trust it yet. I don't trust anything yet.

I am afraid to look over at Susan or even glance in her direction. I want to give her space. I needn't have worried. She was giving herself plenty. It was my own space I should have been concerned with.

The ceremony is broken into three parts, each one accompanied by Aurora's shamanic drumming. Aurora has been working as a shaman for the past sixteen years. As I study her, I realize that I have seen her before. Ithaca is a small place. Ithacan's joke about the one-point of separation that exist between each of us. Jasmina, an energetic healer, will be working with the energy in the room.

Next to each of our blankets is a handout with seven aspects of healing the inner child. The first reads,

For your wounded inner child to come out of hiding, he
must be able to trust that you will be there for him.

He? Him? It shocks me when I come upon it. What is "he" doing here? I didn't invite *him*, and I didn't want *him*. Didn't "He" get enough attention throughout the ages? Wasn't shamanic journeying originally feminine? Weren't we about to make our way into a space more akin to the energy of water and the phases of the moon?

I am outraged. Even more distrustful of this experience after reading this, I look around the room. There are nine of us here about to go on this journey, and only *one* of us is male. Here it is, more evidence of the original wound. Patriarchy, on the page. I gently (not easy since I'm triggered) pull Jasmina over before we start and let her know that the use of the male patronym isn't working for me. She looks bewildered.

"It's just some information that we quickly put together before the workshop," she explains. "It's the first time we've done this, so it's useful to have your feedback. I'll look into that for the next one."

"Thank you," I say. "I've been changing the pronouns as I read it, but it just sort of strikes me that this is reflective of our original wounds, you know?"

I am not sure she knows.

The second aspect of healing the inner child is *Validation*.

If you're still inclined to minimize and/or rationalize the ways in which you were shamed, ignored, or used to nurture your parents, you need now to accept the fact that these things truly wounded your soul.

No wonder there are so few straight, undamaged seeming trees in the woods, I think to myself.

Your parents weren't bad, they were just wounded kids themselves, the handout continues.

My mistrust of this notion of healing one's inner child, makes me ready to reject what is happening here. Then I read:

If you used to nurture your parents, you need now to accept the fact that this truly wounded your soul.

My resistance starts to melt.

Validation is followed by *Shock, Anger, Sadness, Remorse,* and *Loneliness.*

The deepest core feelings of grief are toxic shame and loneliness. We feel shamed by [our parents] abandoning us. We feel we are bad, as if we're contaminated. And that shame leads to loneliness . . .

Toxic shame and loneliness inhabit me on this day. I go through the next two and a half hours feeling like a pariah. I don't realize until later that these feelings have been triggered by my interaction with Susan in the kitchen before the ceremony. Her possible rejection of my presence catalyzed my deepest feelings of unworthiness. It inhabits my body, my psyche, and permeates the room. Certain I don't belong here, my presence is a scourge, a virus, a potential plague. I feel less worthy of this healing than everyone else in the room. Perhaps even everyone else on the planet.

❣

Healing begins when our shadow, the parts of ourselves that feel ugly and bad, take their place at the table.

The first part of the ceremony is the Invocation. During this bit, we invite our inner child to the ceremony, ask her about her trauma, and what wounds she needs to heal.

Unaware that my wounded child is already present, I sit in meditation, and call her forth. To my surprise, my inner child dances before me. Vibrant. Energetic. A nymph imbued with the divine spark. I love her immediately. Beautiful, smart, dynamic, spirited, and sprightly. She is the one who has always shown up for me and for life.

All the while, the me in my body in the room, feels small and insignificant.

At the end of the drumming, Aurora speaks first about *What she got,* in the shamanic world. She speaks of the teachers, the spirit guides, and our souls. She saw the compassionate parent present for all of us. I write furiously in my notebook, not wanting to lose a single sensation I have felt during this part of the process.

In addition to the vibrant inner child showing herself to me, there were tears. The sense that no one was watching her beautiful dance, no one was watching out for her. No one saw her beauty or helped amplify its presence in the world. I notice a physical pain in my stomach, gallbladder, and spleen. My solar plexus is throbbing, as though I have just eaten a foot-long sub and it is stuck in a ball, undigested. The next sensation I notice is the heat radiating up through my chest to my throat. This is rage—fire and heat.

I am trying hard to trust this process, wondering if it was right for me to come here, to be here with Susan so close by.

Is it safe? I wonder. I sense that nowhere is safe and remember that feeling safe is really up to me. It is my job to embody the safe, attentive mother so that the wonderful wounded child can come out to play. I so want her here. Despite her wounds, she is bright and funny and 100 percent loveable. She is me and I am her—and I yearn for us to be safe together. I write to her:

I want you to be safe in this body. I want to listen at that level. I really do. I know I have made mistakes. Hurt you, and I might even accidentally do it again, but you deserve the very, very, very best of me and yourself. I invite you here, to be with me—us—come out and play, cry, or rage.

☙

The second part of the ceremony encourages us to call in spirit and release negative experiences, wounds, and emotions. Before we begin, Jasmina hands me the dark, heavy crystal I've had my eye on. *How did she know?* I make myself a comfortable, body-length cushion to lie on with the blankets and cover myself to stay warm. The drumming starts and I put the crystal on my solar plexus. Jasmina has invited us to put up a hand if we'd like her to come by to do any hands-on work.

I want her to come over more than anything.

I don't raise my hand.

A few minutes into the drumming, Susan starts to sob. It is loud. It fills the space. Echoes off the walls. It comes from her belly, gets caught in her throat as she chokes out the sound. I see Jasmina move over to her, kneel down, and start working on her body. I try to keep my focus inward, but it is a challenge. There is something about the expression of her suffering that gets in my way. I begin to sense Native American energy in the room. A name comes to me. *Girl Who Sees.* I find myself chanting this name with the beat of the drum, while my belly begins to vibrate. I am having strong sensations in my groin and lower abdomen. Heat and vibration.

At the start of the ceremony, Aurora and Jasmina told us to look for signs that energy was moving; tears, sadness, heat, shaking, or vibrations. Energy is definitely moving in me, but my solar plexus still feels stuck. I move the crystal over the various chakras as they speak to me to strengthen the energetic focus on that area. Jasmina comes to stand near me toward the end of this segment. I can feel her clearing the energy that has been stirred up. She steps away, and it all feels heavy again.

Aurora's drumming gets quieter and quieter until it stops. Several successive drumbeats ring out to close this part of the shamanic journey. Jasmina begins by sharing what she got:

"There was a lot of energy about not belonging; there not being enough space for you. It was never your path to fit into society. You have felt rejected, not accepted by people trying to fit you into molds that were never going to fit. I see body parts taken, healed, and brought back. There is some aspect of self-blame, not doing what you think you should be doing. We blame ourselves for not fitting in; we blame ourselves, feel it is our fault. You need to be held as you are without someone trying to make you something else. We are the only ones equipped to heal ourselves in these wounded places."

Aurora speaks next about what she found in the shamanic space. My eyes fill with tears as she shares.

"There was a lot of darkness. Energy and angelic hosts filled the room holding candles and light to clear out the darkness. They were giving unconditional love and healing energy. Another spirit guide was also giving unconditional love. I saw the darkness clearing, the sun came out, flowers were blooming. There were birds . . . It's about self-love now. Our parents did the best they could."

၆၃

We take a break. I sit in the corner of the bench in the kitchen once more, get out the half chicken salad sandwich that Chris has so lovingly prepared and begin to eat. Several people from the workshop have gathered around the tea counter. They are talking loudly and laughing. I hear something about chocolate. Susan is there, and I am overcome again by the sense I don't belong. Didn't she make this clear? Or was this a story I made up? An old reel so familiar, I wear it like skin.

Clearly this was *my* story. The unhealed place that gets so easily triggered.

They all go back into the yoga space, except for Susan. She is cupping her tea close to her chest. The rims of her eyes are swollen and red. Her cheeks are puffy, and she exudes that open-heart feeling you get when you've just cried yourself silly. Released demons from your soul. An empty cauldron filled with presence. Loving presence. She looks at me, sitting in the corner of the bench feeling invisible, nibbling like a mouse on the corner of my sandwich.

"How are you?" she asks.

"I don't know," I answer.

"Um hm." She nods. We linger for a moment, just looking at each other, and she moves on.

Jasmina is at the door peering in.

"Is it bad that I'm eating right now?" I ask.

"No, it's fine."

"I wanted you to work on my third chakra in there."

"Really? I thought so. I don't want to just come over and start working on people's bodies without their permission. But I was getting a lot of signals."

"I could really feel it when you stood over me toward the end of the second segment."

"Yeah. There was some energy that wanted to move. I felt that someone else had left their imprint on you. That it didn't belong to you. I was moving it off you."

A chill ran down my body, head to toe through all four limbs.

"Would you like me to work on you during the third part of the session?"

"I would."

❦

Part three of the healing circle is about receiving guidance from or more healing for the inner child. When the drumming starts, I find myself chanting inside.

Child Who Sees.

Child Who Knows.

She is Me.

Over and over and over, I chant this until Jasmina comes over and places her hands over the center of my rib cage. She works first without touching me, moving energy, then her fingertips touch the area between my breasts. The crystal rolls onto my neck and off to the side. She moves it. She touches me again, very lightly, fingertips over my stomach and back up to my heart. I hear her writing something with one of the crayons next to my mat. Then she moves off, and on to another person.

I chant again, but it no longer rings true.

Child Who Laughs.

Child Who Dances.

Child Who Acts.

Child Who Cries.

Child Who Hurts.

She is Me.

She is Me.

This lonely child, rarely seen, known, or held; feeling scared, alone, and forgotten, she resides in me.

The child,

the child,

the child in me
wants to play freely
without fear.

The drum slows, gets quieter until the three resounding beats followed by four more close this part of the healing. Once again, we are invited to speak.

"There is nothing really to heal but your own perception of your beautiful self," Jasmina reveals.

I am distracted by the last typed sentence on the page. It is under the heading *Loneliness* and describes how we created a false self, to cover up all the shame and loneliness. How the false self hides our shame and loneliness not only from others, but from ourselves as well. The true self remains alone and isolated (very much like the experience I was having in the room—and, oh, is it familiar).

"In embracing our shame and loneliness, we begin to touch our truest self," she adds.

I remember that she has written a message just for me. I look down and see written in purple crayon with wavy water lines on the bottom:

"I remove these swords placed upon me and lay them in the water."

As I begin to ponder what it means, I notice that Susan has gotten up and is standing by the door. I notice this with my peripheral vision, still telling myself that my full gaze is not welcome.

Jasmina continues, "The younger self needs some attention. Check in. Ask yourself, 'How would I treat my daughter or my niece?' Write with your nondominant hand to hear the inner child's voice."

A woman in the room speaks. She is a large woman wearing loose Flax-style clothing. Her head is shaven. I overheard her talking about practicing Tonglen—the Buddhist practice of taking in other's pain and suffering and exhaling joy and lightness—at some point in the day and wonder if she's a Buddhist. She is seventy years old but looks much younger. Her voice is small, but her presence is big.

"I've been asking myself what it is for me, this inner child work. It's not reexperiencing the horror. I've done that. I think it's really experiencing that which I couldn't experience because of the horror. That's the inner child work I want to do now."

Amen sister, I think. *I'll drink to that.*

The imprint left on me from others that is not my own. The sword placed upon me. I lay it in the water.

The sword symbol strikes me as almost too clear. I see the male phallus. I think of the male fingers touching, probing my infant body.

"Take them off of me!" I shout from within. "Get them away from me."

But it's also my mother's hands and her untamed rage. The sudden loss of control. The violence her demons demand. The personality always groping for more space. The flow of words that exit her mouth and push me into a corner.

&#x03G8;

I am the first to leave. I can't get out of there fast enough. A half mile down the road, I realize I have forgotten my lunch box. I turn the car around and head back. Several people are talking to the seventy-year-old bald woman in the hallway. She is holding court. Perhaps she has spoken a truth the others need to hear. I'm secretly hoping that Aria, Susan, or Jasmina will be in sight so that I can say goodbye.

Did anybody notice I had left?

None of them are there, so I grab my lunch box, turn and leave again. Three-quarters of the way home, I realize I have forgotten my water bottle. I don't turn back. All the way home I feel angry. I'm angry at Susan. I blame her for making me feel unwelcome before the ceremony had even begun—the way I blame my mother for making me feel invisible and hurt. I hold Susan responsible for all the negative feelings that hovered around me, keeping me alone throughout the ritual.

My rational mind says, "No." My puny, miserable, lonely self says, "Yes."

I remove the swords placed upon me and lay them in the water.

The water seems too nice a place for the perverted presences that have hurt me and my lineage. Then it occurs to me. *We were all doing our best job.* The babysitters with probing fingers and feather dusters, the men sitting in parked cars with their dicks exposed, the twenty-year-old who needed to jerk off so badly he had to do it in front of two ten-year-old girls getting into their bathing suits in the changing hut next to a pond at the music festival. And my mother.

Especially my mother.

These people who wounded me were wounded themselves. They *too* need the healing waters. They *too* need to be brought back to source. I can't go there and leave them behind. They live in me. This thought soothes me.

But I am still mad at Susan. And my mother.

Chapter Seven

Getting to Know Little Me

*It's okay to be angry, even if what was done to you was unintentional.
In fact, you HAVE to be angry if you want to heal your wounded
inner child. I don't mean you need to scream and holler (although you
might). It's just okay to be mad about a dirty deal.*
John Bradshaw

When I get home, I'm in a foul mood. My insides are on the outside. I
feel raw and dangerous. My husband is playing the cello when I walk
in. He wants me to hear the new song he's been working on. I can't hear
anything.

We take a walk. I am mad. We make dinner. I am mad. We sit
down to eat. I am mad. I am so very utterly mad.

I step back and think, *God damn, this inner child is a pain in the
neck. She is too hard to handle. She is so damn needy.* I can't imagine
having to put up with me.

I hear Jasmina's words. "How would you treat your own
daughter? Or a student at school?"

I decide to try a different approach. My inner child is trying to
communicate with me after all. So what if it is an irrational mess of
barbed wire?

I soften my inner gaze and ask, *What's up little buddy?*

I get my answer right away.

I look out beyond the bleeding hearts and the budding raspberry in the back garden and I see. I feel. I know.

Little me, preverbal me, sexually abused infant me is showing me something I need to understand.

Peter Levine talks of *freezing* as being one of our natural survival responses to trauma. We freeze when any attempt to get away will not work. A baby who is maltreated has only its voice to defend itself. When the voice doesn't stop the unwanted hurt, the soul retreats, forgets how to reach out for help or safety.

In addition to unintentionally triggering my sense of not belonging, of being a freak in this world, Susan triggered this wound—the wound left when the powerful exploit the powerless. My capacity to reach out, to ask for what I needed during the healing ceremony was shut down. How many times did I want something and not ask for it? The crystal, the energy clearing, the sense of belonging.

The infant in me who couldn't speak, who needed others to intuit and respond to her needs came alive. This infant needed desperately for those in power to be paying close attention to the signs and signals necessary for her survival. For my survival. For my protection.

Jasmina, whose job it was to be tuned in, heard the cries of my soul.

When Susan had her powerful release—the loud crying and sobbing that filled the room and seemed to go on for hours—something in me felt violated. An invisible boundary breeched. I was being forced to be present to something intimate and private. Something that should have been happening behind a closed door. I was being invaded, and I couldn't stop it. I felt there was a sexual quality to her deep release. It just kept on coming. Again, and again, like someone else's orgasm. Like the trees at night. I tried to be as small as I could. Or disappear entirely.

Susan hadn't knowingly tried to hurt me; yet, when we saw each other we both asked, "Is this okay?" She went upstairs to contemplate; I stayed downstairs and waited to hear what *she* felt, ignoring the signs in my *own* body saying "no." As my once therapist, as the one who was once in the role to give me guidance, *Wasn't it still her job to know the boundaries that would keep us both safe? Wasn't she the one holding the power here?* A chord of *the* boundary issue I have been grappling with my entire life got struck.

I don't know exactly how I saw all of this when I looked out into the back garden, but it became clear in an instant. When we open ourselves to source and healing, sincerely open ourselves to our own divine light, it will take us where we most need to go.

How could I know or predict how things would turn out? Susan, hooked into the same cosmic intelligence as me, became the catalyst for the healing my soul needed.

I got to experience the child, and Susan got to unknowingly and unintentionally play the role of my initial aggressors. The adult witness, the compassionate parent, and all the spirit guides took part, holding the space for me to have a preverbal encounter with the original sin done before I even had a body or soul or the ability to stop it.

☷

Two days after the workshop, I meet with a writer friend who is a deep empathic listener. Ironically, we sit facing each other under a large statue of Artemis, Greek goddess of the hunt and protectress of the girl child. She stands on an altar filled with a vase of spring flowers.

"How are you?" she asks, eyes a clear shade of blue.

I start to cry the second her gaze falls upon my sorry state.

"About as bad as you can imagine," I say, letting the tears fall, my chest and belly heave; the sobs pour out.

"I'm completely lost," I whimper. "I have no idea what I'm doing or where I am."

I share what happened at the healing ceremony. I share how it stimulated my deepest boundary breeches and allowed me to "see" and feel what had happened to me before I had learned to talk.

"I had a transference," I say, using language I picked up from so many years as the child of a licensed social worker.

Still, I don't know how to proceed.

"I don't have a practice for what is happening now." Wiping my tears, I recall the reaction of my acupuncturist when I told her about what I am writing. She asked if I had the necessary protections to enter this difficult and painful terrain.

"The truth is, I'm not sure I feel safe with myself right now." I continue.

"Why don't we both do a contemplation on that right now? Let's start with the question, 'How can I feel safe with myself?'"

I write whatever comes to my mind:

Listen for the quiet voice; it speaks very softly, almost inaudibly.

Sometimes the child seems like a tyrant. But if I soften my gaze, she usually has something to say or show or tell or share. The trick is knowing how to listen.

When I wish others were listening to me, that's the signal I need to tune in and listen more carefully to myself.

I am surprised by what comes out onto the page. My friend suggests we do a meditation, get quiet, ask for more guidance then begin writing again whenever anything more comes up. Very soon after I get quiet, the child within shows herself. She is sitting nearby. She takes my hand, wants to play, wants to dance. Then we sit. She sits on my lap. I tell her I can listen if she wants to talk. She tells me she isn't sure, but we agree this is what we need to do. Sit together each day for a little while.

To get to know each other and build trust. She isn't just going to give me her trust. I have to earn it. We have to build it together.

I decide that I will spend time each day for a while getting to know my inner child. That I will write when I feel like it, not push myself to write at a certain time each day, even though that has been my practice. I tell this to my friend.

"Good," she says. "Don't *make* it easy. *Let* it be easy."

I invite my inner child to take a walk with me that very afternoon in my favorite local state park. She says yes. But it turns out it isn't all that easy to take a walk with my inner child.

I park in the upper parking lot of the rim trail at Taughannock Park. Taughannock is one of the state parks that the Ithaca area is famous for. It's about ten miles outside of Ithaca on the west side of the lake. The waterfall is taller than Niagara Falls, but depending on how rainy it's been, can range from raging waters to a trickle the size of my pinky finger.

I love this park. I have walked this trail countless times alone, with friends, but most often with Chris. This is the park where we courted for years before we got married. In the early days of our relationship, when I was teaching full-time in a nearby high school and had a free period before and after lunch, we would meet at the park to eat together. Chris would show up with a full picnic for us to share. We would jump over a fence at the top of the rim trail and walk out onto one of the rock promontories that line the gorge's edge. On the exposed surface of rock that was once, long ago, part of the ocean floor, we would turn our faces to the sun, kiss and eat, hug and eat, then kiss and laugh and eat some more. If there was time, we would walk along the rim of the deep gorge, stopping along the way to take in the view down below.

I bring my inner child here. She jumps out of the car as soon as it is parked and begins to run. I follow behind, like a joy-filled, watchful parent. We stop to look at wildflowers and the shape of leaves. Then she is off running down the path again. We hold hands, skip and talk and I explain how some wild plants are medicinal and good to eat. We taste wild garlic mustard and notice plantain growing in tufts along the sides of the trail. She stomps in puddles and sits up on top of fences, securely in my arms of course, to look down into the depths of the gorge and the fast running water at its base.

The sky starts to get dark from the northwest. She notices it and gets scared. I assure her that we will keep an eye on it, but that we aren't in any danger for now. We keep on. We stop for squirrels, to inspect knots in trees and again, take in the view. She starts to get tired, so I carry her on my back. Then, we both have to pee. We squat next to a tall maple that has three enormous trunks growing out of the same base, the middle of which has either been struck by lightning at some point or suffered a nasty disease and won.

Once we are sure it is safe, we both pee at the same time. She finishes first and climbs into the hole in the base of the tree. Again, we trot down the path, but she is getting more and more scared by the sky. I really want to keep walking but remember that I am trying to gain her trust, so we set a point not far down the trail where we will turn around and head back. She bolts to the tree and is back at my side in a jiffy. I keep my normal pace and wish I had brought some Pepperidge Farm goldfish or string cheese to distract her. I can tell she is getting tired and so am I. It has been so many years since I have given a young child my undivided attention. I have forgotten how demanding a child can be.

On the walk back up, I tell her I need a little break. That I need to be quiet for a while. That she can walk but if she is too tired, I will carry her. She gets upset. I feel it. I hold her close to my chest while we walk. She is mad that I need a moment to myself. I explain that sometimes adults need breaks, but that it doesn't mean I don't love and adore her. I let her cry for a long time about this. Eventually, she stops, and we both feel lighter.

She gets into the back seat of the car, and we stay quiet most of the way home.

Chris greets me at the door. I have a lilt in my step. I thought I would still be exhausted, but instead, I am energized. Oh, how I love my little inner one. What a sweet delight she has been, even in her hurt and anger. Especially in her hurt and anger.

I don't share any of this with Chris, but all night long, I am amazed at how little attention I need from him. I go to bed smiling, my little one curled up with me, as close to my heart as she can get. I am starting to earn her trust.

CB

I'm trying out different names for my inner child, since *Inner Child* provokes such a sour taste in my mouth. My acupuncturist suggests "Interior Nipper," but that doesn't seem to fit. I settle on *Little Me* for now.

I go for another walk with five-year-old Little Me. We enter the woods to the north of our property heading toward the YMCA land once used by Primitive Pursuits. Primitive Pursuits is a local wilderness education program for people of all ages. They are partnered with Cornell University and offer programs all year round. This, once one of their campuses, is part of my daily walk.

Shrill screams and gales of laughter fill the air. Little Me's ears perk up. The sound encircles us and bounces down the path all at once. We take the White path and move steadily toward the heart of the cacophony. The ground is wet again, and there are slugs every few inches.

I have always hated slugs. I detest the thin slimy film they leave behind as they move slowly over leaves and grass, back windows, front entrances, and the like. I am especially grossed out when I walk outside barefoot in the dark and step on one. Even the toughest detergent can't get that slime off your skin once it's there.

Not so for Little Me. The first slug we see piques her curiosity. I notice her delight. It is the small, quiet almost imperceptible voice inside that says so.

"Stop," it says. "I want to check this out."

I almost don't hear it, almost pretend it isn't there, but instead, I stop. We stop, turn around, and bend down to take a closer look. The slug is a mix of incandescent yellow and orange with a wet slick body. It moves slowly over the ground, making its way over the edge of a dead maple leaf. It's feelers are out. Crouched on the ground I see how interesting it is; sheer and shrugging slowly from side to side. *Where are they all going?* One slug hovers over a small green stem with tiny leaves. It takes me a moment to realize that it is eating. We linger, poised, our bodies bent with interest. The slug has stopped moving altogether and is taking its time to ingest every bit of the small plant.

"Wow," says Little Me. "That's so cool. I didn't know slugs had mouths on the bottom of their bodies."

"Me either," I reply. We watch and wait a bit more, but a slug really takes its time when eating.

We stand up, and continue down the path. All along the way, we make sure to notice and appreciate every slug.

The loud shrieks get louder.

Then suddenly, there they are. A group of children, aged seven to eleven, are shooting arrows at a series of targets made for this purpose where the Red trail veers off the White toward the Blue. Little Me is intrigued but also scared by the sheer volume of the sound. We slow down to take a closer look. I figure Little Me would like to be part of the group of youngsters exercising the limits of their outdoor voices. There is a somewhat haggard-looking young man leading the group, making sure no one accidentally takes out another's eye.

The teacher in me empathizes with the tired-looking adult. Free spirit me thinks, *Great. These kids have been inside all day long, sitting unnaturally behind desks, fidgeting, waiting to be able to run around, yell, and play. What better place to do this than in the woods?* Woodland mystery lover me thinks, *How will they hear the subtle voice of nature if they spend all their time yelling at the top of their lungs with joy?* I later learn that this wasn't a Primitive Pursuits group, but a YMCA afterschool group out for some fun and games. Still, I wonder, how would a skillful leader go about harnessing all that abundant energy to help it become curious about the quieter, more mystical side of Nature?

Little Me and I keep on walking as I explain some of my thoughts about the wonders and challenges presented by this group. I try to talk to Little Me a lot, explain how I see things working, why people sometimes do the things they do, and what things mean. Little Me didn't get many explanations, so was left to make up her own meaning most of the time. Even though she was smart and gifted, she responded the way any child her age would. Children, naturally egocentric, will interpret most things as having something to do with them, unless they are helped to understand.

Little Me grew up with a distorted view of reality and a distorted view of herself and her own power. When bad things happened around her or to her, she assumed she had somehow abetted if not caused them. She looked at faces, read bodies carefully for the signs and reflections of who she was, but without guidance, often misread a language she didn't understand. How could she know that almost everyone walking around has a wounded inner child looking for the same thing she was, some kind of validation of its own worth? Its own right to stand tall in this world.

Because her parents (my parents I have to remind myself) were particularly wounded as children, they were even less suited to know how to help her grow into and understand herself and the world. She did the best she could given the circumstances, as we all do.

Little Me had no idea how to deal with how scared and unprotected she felt all those years growing up. She hid it from herself. She floated above fear, hid behind the couch, and made faces pretending to scare off a world that left her shaking and alone. It made her brittle over time, and she grew porcupine spikes to protect her secret, and rarely, if ever, let anyone, especially herself, see that tender, vulnerable child who needed care.

Until it started making her sick.

We stop to hug a huge pine tree with rough puckered bark and many arms growing out to hold a child who dares to climb. Up she goes. I give her a boost onto the first branch. She scurries up to the middle of the tree, knees covered in sticky pine sap. She looks down at me, and I up at her. I tell her to not go too high, and I catch her when she jumps back down. Around the next bend, a red-headed pheasant takes off to fly deeper into the woods. We soon come to the Coy Glen stream and I tell Little Me that we might see a red newt if we are very lucky. Big Me wants to head to the right, under the thick shade of the Coy Glen hemlocks. But I hear that subtle voice again that says, "Go left." We go left and soon, there is our first red newt in the middle of the path.

We bend down to investigate. It is bright orange and has four circles on each side of its spine. It doesn't move. Soon, a small white worm pokes its head out from under a soggy brown leaf on an adjacent tree root. We watch for a while, then lift the leaf to see how long the worm is. It is about half an inch. Carefully, we replace the wet leaf to protect the vulnerable white worm.

I explain to Little Me how the red newt likes to keep its body moist, and thus can usually only be seen on wet days like this. We wonder where this newt lives, since it is so far from the stream bed. I touch its tail with a pine needle to try to incite it to move, and it takes two steps toward the edge of the path. Little Me wants to pick it up, but I explain that it gives off a chemical that is toxic to humans, plus we don't want to scare the newt. We stand up, wish the newt a safe journey through the rest of its life, and continue toward the stream.

By the time we reach the stream bed, we have seen at least four more newts. Sometimes the smallest newts have the most spots, which seems backward. Shouldn't the oldest newts have the most spots and be the biggest?

At the stream, I remind Little Me of how she used to spend hours in the creek behind our house in downtown Naples, NY, looking for crayfish. We decide to stop and have a peek. We turn a few rocks before we see it. It backs its way toward the edge of the newly uncovered space, trying to find cover. It is a grayish brown crayfish, the color of the dirty bottom of the creek muddled up with each rock we touched. It has strong looking pincers and its tail is tucked under. I marvel at our good luck. Several days later, when I am on another walk, this time without Little Me, I turn rock after rock in vain in search of our newfound friend. It doesn't reveal itself to me ever again.

Around the bend we go, near the fading trillium and the different varieties of forest fern. Every time we come upon a newt, we stop to inspect it before wishing it a safe journey through the rest of its life.

On our way out of the woods and back toward home, we see a rabbit standing on its hind legs in the center of the clearing. It reminds us of the shape of the solid chocolate Easter bunnies that we would find downstairs on Easter morning growing up. I am holding Little Me's hand

and we stop together for a few breaths. We take several steps toward the bunny before it bounces away through the tall grass.

The honeysuckle is heavy and wet and fills the air with heavenly smells. We get wet as we make our way through the rain-soaked branches hanging in the path. Little Me skips off ahead as I stop to smell the buds.

"Hey, check this out!" I yell. She comes bounding back and I show her how to pull the flower off the honeysuckle stem and suck the nectar from the bottom.

Around the pond, red-winged blackbirds swoop in to land on last year's cattails while crows fly close above our heads. Several swallows hang suspended in a wind current above, forked tails quivering before they dart away. A thick carpet of black tadpoles line the clear edges of the pond.

I think we might have hot chocolate when we get home, but instead, we take a nap with the cat. Well, I nap while Little Me pets the cat.

Chapter Eight

No Idea What I'm Doing

I have no idea how to parent Little Me. I feel like I got lucky the day of the walk. I haven't been able to repeat it since. I'm supposed to be earning Little Me's trust, but I'm so used to behaving like "Big Me" that I don't always know what that means. When I do things during the day, I invite her to join. But I'm usually distracted, by my phone, by the latest Trump drama, by whether North Korea's missile blast was a success and how much longer we have on earth, by what we will eat for dinner, by the weeds in my garden, by so many things.

I apologize to Little Me. Acknowledge my distraction, try to come back. Usually, at this point, I find an angry little girl who wants to hit me. Instead, I pick her up and let her wail in my arms. We walk through the woods this way. Sometimes I lift my arms up and actually hug myself, but only if I know I'm alone. Other times, I just feel myself hugging her sweet little enraged body. She can howl for a long time. I pat her back and just let her do it.

"I know. I'm tired today," I say, and go on to explain that it doesn't mean I don't love her. I go even further and explain that it doesn't mean her parents didn't love her either. They *did*. They always loved her very much. They were just broken and distracted with themselves and all the things they needed to get done all the time.

൫

I was once bulimic. All of this work with Little Me has put me in touch with a pain just below my left rib. It's at the same level as my third chakra, home of the fire that feeds identity and strong emotion. Fierceness. Rage. Bile. Bellicosity. Power.

Perhaps it should come as no surprise that I find so much intense sensation at this location in my body but it does.

Last summer, I received a divination reading from a Tibetan Buddhist Lama. As we sat facing each other, he massaged his mala and spoke. Occasionally, he paused to pray and move the mala through his fingers, one bead at a time. He told me I would become steadily happier as I aged (this was good news) and to be careful the year I turn sixty (pay attention to diet and spiritual practice). He told me that I am rich in creativity, skillful means, and determination. I was really starting to like this guy. He affirmed that I will never get stuck. That I'm smart and when an obstacle arises, I will always see a way out and take it.

Once he finished telling me all about how fantastic I was, he carefully moved me into the darker side of my nature. He did it lovingly, reminding me that we all have a shadow side.

"Be careful with your friends," he said. "Friends will come and go. It is the nature of life. But you need to avoid rage and arguing."

Bingo. He got me.

"Your health is pure," he said, "but your upper body is prone to sickness. This is related to liver and bile."

Got me again.

"You must avoid conflict. It blocks your creativity. It can cause karma and pain to self and others."

I nodded. It certainly wasn't the first time I'd heard my anger was a problem. Chris loves to remind me how quick I am to get angry (perhaps because he is so frequently its recipient). When I moved into the Ecovillage at Ithaca cohousing community over twenty years ago, it became quickly apparent that I needed to get this roaring tiger under wraps if I was going to create sustainable relations with my neighbors.

Tempa Lama went on to say that I should avoid the sun and extreme heat as this will lead to health problems and that I was meant to be a farmer or realtor.

I gave him my white envelope filled with a donation for his center, bowed, thanked him, and moved awkwardly toward the stairs.

Growing up through adolescence, I knew my sister was bulimic. I would find the evidence in the morning floating in the downstairs toilet. My first year of college, I, too, found myself retching over toilet bowls all over campus.

First off, I had never, and I mean never, been exposed to so much food. In our house, the cupboards went quickly bare. My mother went food shopping once a week and when the grapes, orange juice, and ice cream ran out (often on the very first day), we would have to make due until the next paycheck. At college, the endless buffets of every sort of food you could imagine stretched out before me as if I'd gone to food heaven. I piled my plate high. Went back for seconds. Never left the dining hall without a soft serve twist ice cream on a cone.

Naturally, I began gaining weight. As a long-distance runner, I had always been one of the thinnest people in my class. Gaining weight was something I had never before encountered. Whose body was this anyway?

I was growing up. Leaving home. Becoming an adult. On my own for the first time. And, I had no idea who I was. Growing up, I hadn't learned to recognize a single emotion I was having as mine—my feelings were just a ball of confusion I had no resources to unwind. Now, a freshman in college, I was entirely without the necessary skills to adapt to this monumental change.

I'm not sure how it began, but by the end of my freshman year, I had scoped out every bathroom with a lock on campus and would head there directly after lunch to stick my finger down my throat. This continued for a good year without me ever telling anyone about it.

Anyone who has studied eating disorders knows that it's about control. The inner chaos I had kept at bay for so many years by throwing myself fully into thriving at school, began to lurk close to the surface. The false self I had created began to crack and split. Without my mother present, without the world I had worked so hard to hold back behind the dam, those demons began to come forth. And they wanted to be fed, but I had no clue how. So, I stuffed myself, binge fed anything I might be feeling, then released it by purging it all into the toilet bowl.

At the start of my junior year, I found a therapist. My mother had connections since she had begun her private social work practice by then and helped me find a counselor. Maggie had an office where she would see clients once a week in downtown Ithaca. I saw her for over a year every Wednesday. Never, not once, did I tell her about my bathroom escapades. Instead, I talked about my mother.

I decided I needed therapy the night after I hit my boyfriend. He was much older than me and we had begun living together that summer. He was a waiter at the restaurant where I was working as hostess. One night, we partied hard together. He abandoned me at some point, leaving me alone at the party hosted by one of his friends where I knew no one. When I managed to find my way home, I found him passed out on the couch on the porch outside the second story entrance to our apartment.

I was drunk and high and I flew into a blinding rage. Something primitive got struck by being abandoned at the party, and I came at him with the force of thunder. There was no recovery for us from that. He was not my soulmate. I was nineteen turning twenty. Things were falling apart in my psyche faster than you can eat the perfect hand-cut french fry.

So, I began to consult with Maggie.

Maggie had an eating disorder herself, or rather always seemed to be struggling with her weight. She kept sugar-free Tic Tacs on the table next to her chair and would pop them into her mouth intermittently throughout our sessions. She let me know she was trying to keep her mouth busy so that she wouldn't eat. She was very traditional in her approach, and didn't let me in much on who she was beyond this woman listening while I sat on her couch.

It wasn't until I found myself in France as an exchange student second semester of my junior year, that things turned around for me. Almost overnight, my bulimia became a thing of the past. Immersed in the language and culture of my dreams, something inside me awoke from a deep sleep. For the first time in my life, I felt safe in my body. I couldn't put a finger on what it was exactly that was different, but at no point during my time studying and living in Avignon, did I ever feel as if I were sexual prey walking down the street. One day, I even wore overalls in the city center without a shirt and felt completely secure. (I would never do that now, but I was twenty and experimenting with my bohemian self.)

Naturally, I hypothesized: *It must be the way the feminine is revered in this culture,* I thought, *or the natural seat of power the woman has that is distinct from that of a man.*

Men in France are not afraid of their feminine side. In Paris, it is common to spy an effeminate looking straight man wearing a soft pastel scarf around the neck. Men aren't afraid to touch each other and don't present themselves with the same manly front I was so unconsciously accustomed to. My body relaxed deeply, and I forgot all about the secret art of blowing the day's catch in a remote bathroom.

Now, as I invite Little Me into my daily life, my stomach aches all the time. *Were the demons that had caused me to binge and purge still lurking?* I put my hands on my stomach during a recent therapy session.

"What's going on there?" Joel asks.

"That's where the pain is," I say.

☙

I don't always know how old Little Me is when we're together. Five-year-old Little Me wailing on my shoulder can suddenly transform into one-and-a-half-year-old me. The essence of the grief remains the same, but the size of the body changes. The feelings move through as energy. There is no real content attached; however, they have an essence that is both familiar and new.

Last Saturday, I woke up feeling depressed.

"I seem to remember you feeling that way last weekend, too," Chris reminds me.

I have decided to take breaks from writing on the weekends. This leaves me feeling lost when I wake up on Saturdays. I decide I will go to Lahki to do yoga with Demi. In the bathroom preparing my neti pot before leaving, I talk to Little Me.

"Little Me," I say, "I'm not going to do my usual practice with you today. I'm going to take you to yoga instead. How does that sound?"

I don't really listen for an answer since I'm not ready for Little Me to foil my plans. During the week, I started my morning practice with Little Me each day. She sat in my lap while I meditated, and then she used the 152-count Ultimate Crayola Crayon set while I moved through my asanas.

Today, I think, is a day for me.

A day off.

Little Me will have to tag along.

ɑ

In the parking lot after class I chat with my friend Marge about a love gone wrong. I make space for her heart and she softens right into my energetic embrace. Little Me and I drive off feeling content to have done yoga and been there for a friend in need.

Or so I think.

I take Little Me with me to the Farmer's Market. I need to buy curly kale starts for the garden and more greens for smoothies and salads for the week. It is Cornell graduation weekend, which has made the market particularly crowded, so I am not in the mood to dillydally, something Little Me would have liked very much. All business, we are in and out in under twenty minutes. I can feel Little Me is pouting in the car all the way home.

We come home to Chris, in the kitchen, frying up russet potatoes and last week's local Autumn Harvest Farm bacon. The breakfast is stunning, most every ingredient local, including the toast made with bread from our weekly Wide-Awake Bakery bread CSA. *This is turning out to be a glorious day,* I think. Except it isn't. I can't shake the heavy, depressed, lonely feeling I woke up with. It is haunting me.

I garden. I pull out spent forget-me-nots to make space for the kale starts. Neighbors stop by to chat as I work. The sun even comes out for about twenty minutes. Still, that nagging sensation lurks behind my ears, covers my head, shrouds my eyes.

I drink too much at dinner that night. We have ventured out, Chris and I, for our weekly Saturday night date. Despite the Cornell Graduation families with reservations, we find a seat at the bar of one of our favorite local restaurants. The owner always tries his best to get me drunk when we go. Most times I comply. He starts me with a heavy pour of Highland Park served on my favorite large ice rock. Then has me taste the end of a bottle of Cabernet Sauvignon from a local

Seneca Lake Vineyard. As we are preparing to go, he pours me a dram of Ardbeg.

"Just for the road," he says with a smile.

By the time we get home, my head is spinning.

But it was fun, right? Yes, it was fun. I felt snuggly and close to my husband as we sat side by side for two hours at the bar sharing food. For a while, under the influence of the alcohol, I forget I am feeling bad. We settle in for a night-time episode of *Velvet*, a popular Spanish telenovela and a short brandy (the men in the show are always drinking some form of brown liquor, and it makes it hard not to join in on a Saturday night viewing).

Somewhere toward the middle of the night, I wake up dehydrated. A strong liquor flavor emanates from the back of my throat. I finish the mug of Sleepytime tea on my nightstand and roll onto my belly. The existential crisis begins.

Who am I?

A series of thoughts flow through my head, spiraling me downward toward annihilation. Each new thought brings me closer to my innate nothingness.

I could disappear right now, I think, *and no one would even notice.*

Little Me, is that you? I wonder in the night.

There is no separation between Little Me and Big Me. We are one, and I am feeling bad. I don't try to run or hide or pretend it isn't happening. I just stay here, in pain and tremendous discomfort wondering if I will ever again join the land of the living.

In the morning, I tell Chris how I was feeling in the night.

"Is that your inner child?" he asks.

I laugh. I haven't told Chris much about Little Me. I'm keeping our relationship mostly private for now, curious about how it works and what Little Me really wants.

"I love you," he says, and I know he means that he loves all of me, the lost soul in the night and the beautiful lover of the day. I fall asleep in his arms until we both stir again around 9:00 a.m.

"Okay Little Me. Let's go sit together."

I prepare my meditation space by lighting a rose-scented candle and burning some Palo Santo, a sacred tree often burned in shamanic healing sessions. I say hello to the three *Apprentice Cards,* on my altar: "Clear Flight," "Embody, share your knowledge," and "Enticement into sensory pleasures." *Apprentice Cards* are a sort of nature-image Tarot deck made by a woman photographer seer. I sometimes play with the cards when I start my morning practice. The three cards on my altar accompany me when I write. They hold Spirit and act as visual reminders of support and supplication on this journey. I douse them with a plentiful dose of Palo Santo smoke before I clear my chakras, taking great care to begin and end with my root chakra.

A bright wave of love surges forth as soon as I sit on my pillow. It is as if Little Me is rejoicing, dancing within and without me, inducting me with resplendent light.

"You felt neglected yesterday, didn't you?" I ask, wondering if this was the source of the dark cloud that tracked me all day long.

Within moments, Little Me is sobbing again. I hold her and let her cry. I tell her how much I love her, how sorry I am that she was so sad, so hurt. She lets it roll, doesn't hold back. We sway. Tears fall from my eyes at the pure beauty of it—at this opportunity to give myself the love and attention I have been so craving throughout all of my days in this body.

We hang out this way for a long time. I dedicate my morning meditation to Little Me and she is grateful. When she gets quiet, so do I, and we fall into a very silent, peaceful meditation.

"You need me to start my day with you, don't you?" I ask. She nods vigorously.

I am learning about how to care for my inner child, but really, most of the time, I have no idea what I'm doing. I consider reading John Bradshaw's book or looking into one of the many blogs available online on the topic, but it is such a personal experience. I really want it to be mine, ours.

For now, I resist the temptation to look for guidance from anything beyond myself. I want to explore. To fuck up. To communicate. To listen. To confront myself at every turn. To struggle to be gentle and kind with Big Me as Little Me ventures to show me the way, especially when I fail to listen. I want to have the courage to feel it all as it comes and to get lost and found along the way. And to have a little whiskey now and then.

Just a little.

Just enough.

Right Little Me? *Little Me?*

ଔ

Chris and I make love later that same day. Is it because I gave her all that attention that our lovemaking feels so new?

"I'm going to have some adult time with my husband now. You can run along and play. There's no need for you to hang around for this."

Off she goes.

We begin by sitting together on the bed and joining our breath. Soon enough, though, I am ready to share my body. I want the sensation I can feel with my love.

I am so accustomed to the child in me throwing a tantrum and saying *no*, that I have rarely explored the adult me saying *yes*.

I find myself saying *yes, yes, yes*.

And it is different.

And it is lovely.

&#x08;

Several days later, around 3:00 p.m., after pretending to nap, I decide to get up. The sky is dark, threatening rain. I check the weather on my phone. It's hard to tell what will transpire in the next two hours. I decide to spend a few more minutes in bed and open my *Psychologies* magazine to the focus article on Catherine Deneuve. Now seventy-three years old, she doesn't have a single wrinkle on her face. Deneuve is the actress who played Séverine Serizy in the film *Belle de Jour*, the character who, sexually molested as a child, goes on to tragically live out her masochistic sexual fantasies in a brothel.

Ah, the mysteries of the healing process, I think. *The very serendipity of it all.* First Hélène's query to Claude Halmos, now the actress who played the role in the controversial film that speaks to me so personally. All in the same month's review.

After finishing the article, I decide to take the risk and head to my favorite walk at Upper Buttermilk, another local state park with waterfalls. I call Chris on my way. He is too busy going to Wegmans (local food mart extraordinaire), the bank, and putting up posters for his cello festival to join me for a walk.

When I hang up, my heart hurts. I am surprised by how rejected I feel. The emotion is strong. It fills my chest.

I call him back, tell him how I'm feeling. He drops everything to take a walk with me. When I pick him up downtown the sky is blue.

I am a ticking time bomb. I sense that at any moment, the strong feelings elicited by healing work I received the day before—work done with an energy healer to release the harm done from early childhood sexual abuse and who warned me, "This may bring up some feelings,"—could erupt.

I only hope that I can contain them so as to do no harm.

CB

We walk the lake path like two gentle souls. We hold hands, hug, stop for beauty. But my head is aching. The storm is coming.

Cascades of flowering trillium along the trail make this one of my favorite walks at this time of year. We are about one week too late, however. All the trillium flowers have wilted and hang disenchanted and rotten from below their diamond shaped leaves. We spy a great blue heron eating a fish she has caught in the sinuous stream that runs through the wetland, which was once a deep lake. Time, runoff, and sediment have filled this watery tract, making it a perfect location for birdwatching.

And lovers. This walk is a perfect place for lovers.

Baleful skies alternate between patches of perfect blue, pelting rain, delicate showers, and merciless hail. We take our chances. We stop to watch the blue heron make her way across the rushing water and to watch the moving head of an orange-legged millipede.

Toward the end of our walk, it begins to rain again. We steady ourselves, safe under the heavy canopy of trees, as we make our way out of the woods and back onto the gravel path toward the parking lot. As we descend toward our car, a young family emerges from the lower picnic area next to the turbulent stream. They come up over the lip, onto the grass next to the paved parking lot.

First, a rotund, tall, bald-headed man with a white pit bull on a short leash. Then, a young blond toddler who has clearly recently learned to walk, followed by a full-bodied woman in a tight t-shirt and faded jeans. The adults each take a wrist and balance the young one up and down, swinging him backward as they walk toward their beat-up Buick sedan. I hear no laughter from the child. His body even looks stiff (am I projecting?). Still, I marvel at this scene.

This little one cannot see where he's going. Does he trust that his parents will take him where he needs to go?

By now, Chris and I are in the car, with me driving. We have pulled out and begun our way out of the parking lot on the winding road out of the park. I can't take my eyes off this child. Soon, the parents are talking next to the opened backdoor of the car and the boy is running full steam back toward the path leading to the lower picnic area and the roiling waters.

"Look, look!" I yell, head cocked anxiously over my right shoulder.

Neither parent is paying attention, and it won't be long before this infant is tumbling down the path or being carried off by the wildness of the stream. I am ready to jump out of the car to save him.

"Hey!" Chris says, "Watch where you're going."

In my haste to not lose sight of the boy, I have driven off the road onto the grass. As I pull the car back onto the tarmac, I see the mother running like mad after her child.

"Whew," I say, and I drive slowly on, through the stream as it rushes across the road, among the poplars and the pines that line the road all the way to the exit.

"I'm worried about that boy," I say. "I want to protect him."

The image of the ruined car coupled with the tension in the young boy's body and the struggle I read in the premature creases on the faces of the parents have filled me with dread.

"So much can happen in a life."

What future awaits this innocent child? I wonder. I am thinking of myself. Wishing, praying that this boy will have a safer passage than I did. That he will be spared the early loss of innocence. I know I can't protect him from the assault of life any more than I could have protected myself when I was the most vulnerable.

The rain begins to pour down. It pounds the roof of the car. The sky opens once again, as does my heart.

"Do you want to pull over so I can hug you?" Chris asks.

I am sobbing. Heavy pulses of grief heave up from the depths of memory, blurring my vision. Hurt and betrayal move through my adult body.

"No, I'm okay." I say.

And I am.

ભ

A few days later, Chris and I walk the land that surrounds our community once again. Ecovillage at Ithaca houses three clustered neighborhoods on 178 acres. There are two community sustained agriculture farms, a budding permaculture farm, several neighborhood gardens, and miles of prairie and wooded paths to enjoy. Our property abuts another, smaller intentional community called Long House to the south, and we walk freely on each other's land. The YMCA and Cornell Plantations own woods that border ours. In the winter, we ski the trails for hours at a time. Every other season, we walk, varying our itinerary from day-to-day.

This land is my constant companion. Scarcely a day goes by that I don't find myself deep in its woods. I have come to know its contours. The thicket of white pines and the parcel of birch with their leaves that wave hello in the wind. The way the sugar maples compete with the oaks. The sound of the squirrel that scurries up the trunk and jumps, flies from branch to branch. The vast variety of birds, winged creatures whose songs permeate my every step.

Today, we have taken the gorge trail. Part of the Cornell Plantations land, the middle is cut by a stream that turns into a gorge further down. The land is moist from several days of rain, and the air is cool. Chris precedes me on the trail, which allows me to stay close to myself and my own thoughts. When I lead, often his presence behind me propels me forth, like the mermaid at the bow of the ship. I break through each moment of newness just before he arrives.

"Hey look!" I say as I bend down. We have just walked over the stream that gurgles its way through the rocks, the violets, and the occasional skunk cabbage. The same stream where Little Me and I found the crayfish. The trillium have faded as the ferns slowly unroll their long leaves. Foliage fills the tree canopy overhead.

"What is it?"

"You almost stepped on it."

Chris doesn't tend to notice the red newts the way I do. Also known as an eft, the newt is barely noticeable as it alternately moves its four legs over the dead leaves in the path. I watch it lumber and toil to surmount the vast uneven terrain. Out of the water to feed, it makes its way slowly. At any moment, its life could be taken, by a bird, a fish, a leech, a hungry mammal, the bottom of a hiking boot. From the larval stage to full adulthood (three years), this creature's life is riddled with danger. A full life cycle is between twelve to fifteen years, but how many red newts make it that long?

I see myself in this newt. I see all of us in this newt. The trajectory of our lives is no different. None of us is guaranteed safe passage. Just as this newt could at any moment be besieged by a predator or a passerby meaning no ill will, but simply not paying attention, our lives are at the mercy of so many factors outside our control. From day one, conception to grave, we, too, are creatures living amid the precarious forces of Nature.

"It's dangerous for them to be crossing the path," says Chris.

"Yes. But what choice do they have? They have to eat."

The risks of this existence are so many. We, too, must cross a road of uncertainty if we are to keep growing.

Chapter Nine

Zain

Eight days after my son was born in France, I returned to the states. The story of my precipitous departure is hard to tell. It is another time in my life filled with wonder and pain.

I discovered I was pregnant in July 1996 while my folks were visiting me in France. I had gone there upon finishing my master of arts degree in teaching to be with Frédéric, who I was madly in love with. I had met Frédéric in Ithaca while he was finishing a post-doctoral program at Cornell University.

I got a job teaching English in Paris and decided to stay in France for a while to nurture our relationship. Since he was living and working as a researcher in political and social science for the French government in St Etienne, a city an hour to the southwest of Lyon, we saw each other on the weekends. Soon into our weekends together, I noticed something was not quite right. Frédéric's moods and behavior were erratic. There was a dark shadow surfacing in him that I had never seen during our time together in Ithaca. Sometimes, when he was speaking, his thoughts would wander into a land I could scarcely follow or understand. It was getting more and more unpredictable and strange until I was on the verge of cutting things off between us.

That, of course, is when I learned I was pregnant.

Despite the uncertainty in my relationship with Frédéric, becoming a mother was crystal clear.

I loved being pregnant. Each day I would meditate and ask for protection for the child growing inside my belly. The miracle of life happening within had me constantly mesmerized. Meanwhile, Frédéric's condition worsened. I had no idea what was wrong. I was isolated in France. With few friends and no family, Frédéric was my only support as I was embarking on the biggest adventure of my life. This became even more true upon leaving my job in Paris to join Fred in St. Etienne when I was four months pregnant. As the pregnancy progressed, so did Fred's symptoms and my sense of isolation. By the time I was giving birth, I could scarcely have him in the room, so difficult had his presence become to me.

My mother, at her best in times of crisis, helped save the day.

She came to town to lend a hand four days after our son Zain was born. By then, Fred had become dangerous. He had started covering Zain's head with a blanket in the night and would become enraged when he needed to be breastfed. One night at dinner, Frédéric got up and pulled everything off the shelves into a pile in the middle of the floor. My mother and I just looked at each other. The next night when he stood with the baby in his arms in front of the open window—our apartment was on the fourth floor—we looked at each other again.

"Marcy, I understand now what you've been talking about on the phone," my mother said to me while Frédéric was in the bathroom. "I'll do anything you need to help."

The next day, while Fred was at work, we booked our tickets back to the states. *What role did my unresolved trauma play in creating another traumatic event in my life?*

℘

Frédéric got the care he needed in France after we left. He was having a psychotic break and was hospitalized and placed on a medication that helped him rediscover his normal. It was a gut-wrenching time for all of us, but my mission was clear—protect at all costs and safely mother this new life that had come through me.

The call came one morning while Zain and I were still sleeping in the basement of my mother's house. The clinic in France where Zain was born had been looking for us for a month. They had some bad news. The results of one of the blood tests they had done after Zain was born had come back elevated.

Three months later, through genetic testing, we learned that Zain had Duchenne muscular dystrophy. Duchenne muscular dystrophy is a genetic muscle-wasting condition. It is the most serious form of muscular dystrophy there is. This news changed the course of my adult life and would go on to color every aspect of my existence. This ongoing chapter of my life is its own epic tale and adventure.

The mutation that caused Zain's Duchenne happened when my body was developing inside my mother's womb—the womb of a body that had known sexual trauma. All the eggs that would one day exit my body through menses or in the form of a child, were made while I was growing in my mother's uterus. It is likely that a small group of my eggs, when being formed, missed out on the genetic coding to make healthy muscle. The geneticist we worked with described it like making a photocopy.

"Sometimes there is a little fold in the original on the glass and not all the material ends up on the copy," she said the day the genetic results came back. Zain, three months old at the time cooed in his stroller while I pinched my skin to stay present and comprehend what it all meant.

It is likely that only one of my eggs held this genetic difference and that egg became Zain.

There is really no way to understand the odds of this other than to ascribe it to Fate. Somehow, my mother and father's story, and their mother and father's stories and so on, back fourteen generations, as well as my story and Zain's father's and his family's stories, live on in and through Zain. The stories of our families continue on, only this time, they are made visible to the world in Zain's body. The history of so many people "learning to walk," the imprint of trauma and success, roll through Zain's body as he rolls through his days, just as it does in mine.

But, oh, how I wish Zain could have been spared. That the struggles and suffering familiar to so many of us in this family lineage could have somehow skipped over the genetics of my son. *How angry this bum deal can make me.*

Despite the inevitability of chance, fate, genetics, and a multigenerational lineage of happenings that aren't my fault, I still feel guilty.

What mother wouldn't?

ᘒ

Zain and I found our way to Ithaca and set ourselves up as renters at the newly built Ecovillage. While we set up our new life together, my mother and her psychologist friends found me another therapist. In addition to being skilled as a social worker, Brenda was a writer and an herbalist. I consulted with her for over ten years.

The first three years of being a mother were more exhausting than anything I could have imagined. I was a single mother teaching French and Spanish full-time to middle schoolers an hour away while still breastfeeding a ten-month-old baby. I weighed 122 pounds, the lightest I'd been since running cross country and track in high school.

During those first years of therapy, we began each session with an account of how I planned to take care of myself that week. I lined up babysitters to give myself time off. I got acupuncture every Friday before picking Zain up at daycare. I would take a day off work every few weeks just to rest while Zain was at daycare.

My main goal, besides putting food on the table, was to be the best mother I could possibly be to Zain. Isn't it natural to want to protect our children from the harm that was done to us? I protected Zain fiercely by being as emotionally present and available as possible. I endeavored to be open and communicative, much like I am now with Little Me, so that Zain never had to think that he was responsible for what I was feeling. Where my mother had failed me, I would attempt to succeed with Zain. I did my best to be an attentive, loving mother and Zain flourished.

It helped tremendously that my mother supported me emotionally and financially at every turn during this time of single parenting. Zain, spoiled by the attention and gifts lavished on him by his grandmother, received the attentive grandmother my mother wished she could have been with my sister and me growing up.

Stability comes when it comes. My mother had found her own ground by now and was more able than ever to join us in this new life. It was a beautiful time for us.

While I processed in therapy what it meant to be the mother of Zain, I don't remember it much. Mostly, I continued to talk a lot about my relationship with my mother and the ways my own spotty development would affect other areas of my life. I made huge progress.

When Zain was two, Frédéric came to visit for the first time. We discovered we were still very much in love. When Zain was three, we got back together and spent the next few years mostly happy. When Zain was five, Frédéric learned that his tenure as a Visiting Scholar at Cornell would soon come to an end. The bottom of a marriage that was still struggling to build a foundation, fell out completely. Because of the trauma, isolation, fear, and abandonment I experienced during my pregnancy in France, I wasn't able to envision myself moving back.

Enter Chris.

Chris waltzed right through the cracks in my marriage as they opened irreparable and wide.

"You think you're growing an orange tree and it turns out to be apple," said one of my teachers from the local philosophy center where I had been studying for the past ten years. He was right. As my first marriage was ending, new possibility was blossoming with the man who now shares my life.

Through all of this change, I continued seeing Brenda.

By year ten, the one-and-a-half-hour drive to Brenda's home office each week, then every other week, then once a month, was becoming less and less worth the fifty minutes on Barbara's couch. We loved each other; it was clear. It was also becoming clear that it was time to move on. We had gone as far as we were going to go together.

Was I healed? In many ways, yes. Brenda was a loving pillar during a time of great upheaval and change in my life. She helped me develop a fierce dedication to myself so that I may care for my son, my students, my new husband, and his developmentally disabled daughter. I have tremendous gratitude for the time we spent and the work we did together.

Was there more work to do? Was there hidden trauma that still needed to be healed?

Clearly.

അ

"What's up doc?"

I can hear Bugs Bunny's voice when I read it. "Ba dee, ba dee, ba dee . . ." he says while chewing on a carrot.

I am in my weekly Thursday morning writing group, and I pulled a small piece of paper with these words on it.

If only it was so simple, I think. Cross your legs, lean your hand on a tree trunk, and nibble the end of a fat carrot while you talk.

Maybe it is that simple, if you're a Zen master.

Yesterday I got caught up. In a flurry of worry. My whole day was consumed by it.

My son Zain, now twenty years old, spends his days sitting in an electric wheelchair and long nights in the same position on his back in his bed. He has developed a pressure sore.

It's not the first one. He had one on the under skin of his right forearm where he leans much of his weight throughout the day on the armrest of his chair. He had one on the top of his left foot, where a seam in his Bear Claws slipper was rubbing on the big toe knuckle.

While troubling, both spots were remedied. We got Zain a different pair of shoes. After about six weeks, the toe knuckle calmed down. We padded the arm of his chair, pasted Dr. Scholl's donut bandages around the sore on his arm to take the pressure off. In a few weeks, it was healed.

This new sore, however, is very troubling. It is located on his coccyx in his butt crack just above the anus. It is a small hole, the size of the end of my pinky finger. I know because I look at it. At first, I think, no big deal. It's so small. Zain's aide, Michel, shaves the area around it, to allow us to get a closer look.

My stepfather, who is a dermatologist, tells us over the phone, "If you can't see the bottom of the sore, it could be bad news."

The small hole is filled with pus or Vaseline, or both, so I can't be sure of its depth. Its proximity to Zain's point of elimination means we must be very careful to keep it clean and clear of bacteria. Michel cleans the area, covers it with a generous dose of triple antibiotic cream, and a large, square gauze bandage.

I go home. Except I am not home. I barely notice the sweet taste of mint tea on my tongue that night as I sip it slowly. I experience no elation as Ana and Alberto dance with the impossibility of their love in season four of *Velvet*. Once in bed, my eyes cross over Isabelle Allende's words in Spanish. *Zorro* will have to wait.

What if he never heals?

This is really not the right question to be asking yourself as you settle down to sleep.

He needs to get off that spot, I think as Chris turns out the light.

But it's nearly impossible.

The walls begin to crumble. Structures, fragile at best, have no hold on the tremors of the night.

Could this lead to septic shock? I wonder and toss and turn.

Slowly, yet surely, the health and physical integrity of my son begin to unravel before my closed eyes. It isn't as if this is a novel scenario. When your son is born with Duchenne muscular dystrophy, looking into the future is utterly terrifying, each stage a loss in strength and physical function. Zain, at age four, started falling a lot. Then he stopped being able to run. The neuromuscular specialist, Dr. C., put him on the highest dosage of prednisone his body could tolerate to try to help him preserve motor function. By the age of eight, Zain used a motorized scooter purchased by generous neighbors to get to friends' houses in the village. At age twelve, he needed a wheelchair to walk to the car. His senior year, Zain missed two months of high school when he had nineteen inches of steel surgically adhered to either side of his spine to keep it straight.

And then there is *the skin*.

When the skin starts breaking down, we have entered new territory.

As Michel and I work together to turn Zain on his side and tend to his wound, I notice something else. The skin on his lower back.

Next to the long pale scar that separates the two sides of his mole-covered back are pink splotches of fungus. Nothing new. He has a cream for that. The dark scaly skin around the base of his spine is new to my eyes.

How long has it been since I looked so closely at my son's *skin*?

He moved out of our house to start living independently thirteen months ago at his request. A skilled team of aides and a live-in caregiver make this possible.

For the first six months after he moved out, I was depressed. I had never once, in all my years of advocacy for Zain and people with disabilities, envisioned him leaving our home.

How shortsighted of me.

But the past few months, as I have entered fully into this healing and writing journey and new phase of my adulthood, I find myself smiling a lot. For the first time in my life, the focus is *truly* on me. This is no easy feat in a culture like ours, where such focus is considered selfish. Especially when you're a woman. Even less easy when you are a full-time teacher and have a child and a stepchild with special needs.

As I start my days now with my practice, morning meditation, contemplation, and reading followed by forty minutes of yoga, breakfast, and a few hours of writing, I hear myself say things like, "I really like my life."

Not knowing what the future will bring or how long I will be able to offer myself this luxury, I assiduously protect this daily routine.

"For now," I say. "Always for now."

Though I see Zain four days a week at our house for dinner, I am amazed at how out of touch with the rigors of his daily life and the rigors of being his caretaker I have become since he moved out.

Just yesterday, a neighbor passing by while I was on the phone outside looking at my garden touched my arm and said, "You are a ray of sunshine my dear."

And I was. I am.

As I immerse myself in myself and in healing, I find myself laughing more easily, thinking of my husband's needs more often, delighting in the sound of birds, and stopping to talk to newts.

Has my son's move toward independence freed me up to experience my own and in a whole new way?

On Monday, as I am writing about a challenging time in my life, I feel the impulse to write about my son. I pause.

"This memoir is about me," I say, as I push the impulse back and keep writing.

"He wants to come in," a writer friend says. "Hold your writing loosely."

"This memoir is about me," I repeat. "I know I need to write about Zain, but now isn't the time."

"Why isn't it the time?"

She looks at me, pen poised above her pad.

"Because since Zain moved out, I don't feel close to it."

Suddenly I am lost, dropped somewhere in the labyrinth without a clue where I am or how to get out. The hook in my heart just got tugged. A strangling hold takes over my throat.

I can't breathe, I think, as I bristle and prepare for the deluge.

That night, sitting on the toilet, my head is spinning. I look down at the swirling figures made by the knots in the pine wood slats of the floor. Out of nowhere, death arrives. It hits me in the head, almost knocks me off the seat. Panic. This bolt of lightning fills me with dread.

I can't move.

The imminence of death, my son's death, my own death, sits on top of me while I paw at the toilet paper.

Damn it! I cry. *I want to rest in the field of poppies. Turn stones in search of crayfish. Why can't you leave me alone? Just let me be. Don't I deserve some peace? Haven't I earned this time for myself?*

My creative work sits on a pile of artificial stability. Until this new crisis with my son is sorted out, I am at its mercy.

"Zain," I say later on the phone. "We need to make healing this sore a priority. It needs to be what we're about right now."

"I know, Mom. I think we have a plan."

Zain has done some research and bought an egg carton-styled mattress pad to take the pressure off the area while sleeping. He and his aides are turning him at the start of the night and first thing in the morning before he gets up. Three times a day, they apply the antibiotic ointment prescribed by my dermatologist stepdad and Zain's grandpa, Dappy. Dappy is coming to town in a few days and will have a look at the sore then.

In the meantime, I worry.

"I was thinking maybe you should move home for a while so Chris and I can take turns moving you through the night."

"Mom, I think maybe you're overreacting. Let's try this plan first and see how it goes."

"Okay," I say as we hang up.

Then I call my mother.

☙

My role as Zain's mother has been the focus of my life for the past twenty years. So many of the decisions I made were about and for him.

Take my work in public education.

Before Zain was born, I was living and teaching English in Paris, France. When we returned home, I worked for two years at the college level, teaching English to speakers of other languages. I taught French in the French Immersion program at the State University of New York at Cortland for a semester and loved it. None of these jobs was secure. None offered health insurance or the promise of longevity.

I took a job teaching at the Ernie Davis Middle School in Elmira. There, I taught French and Spanish five days a week to a rough batch of students, many who had a parent in the local maximum-security state prison. I commuted two hours a day, leaving Zain off at daycare before the break of dawn and picking him up in the dark.

But we had health insurance and a regular paycheck, food on the table, and a home in a thriving, growing cohousing community where neither of us would have to be alone.

Or so I thought.

On Saturdays, I would stand looking out the glass window of our front door watching the world go by while Zain played on the floor. I was exhausted. Bone-tired. There was still shopping and laundry and cleaning to do. There was still food to prepare for lunches for the week.

Tears would fall from my single-mother eyes as I longed to just walk out and have a conversation. But I was too tired.

Fortunately for me, this period didn't last.

Not so for my son.

Being born with Duchenne muscular dystrophy means your life is going to be dramatically different from those you grow up with. Being dramatically different foretells a kind of isolation not easily overcome. This has certainly been the case for Zain.

Not having the strength to run or climb or explore the woods with your friends at an age when young people haven't developed the skill of compassion means being left behind time and again. He watched as the friends he once spent all his time with ran by in a pack, not stopping by to invite him to join.

Living in a wheelchair is inherently isolating. It creates a physical barrier to the rest of the world. At school, while Zain's peers would lie all over each other at the weekly All School Meeting, bodies touching, he sat physically apart. While his friends went over to each other's homes at all hours of the day, he often couldn't get up the front steps, much less in their front doors.

When you live in a wheelchair, you are constantly bumping up against other people's unconscious psychological and perceptual barriers, the programming that incites fear. Without even being aware, people are often either too nice (and fake, which drives Zain crazy) or too freaked out to come close to Zain. They struggle to see the person in the wheelchair.

Not once was Zain invited to party with his friends during high school (granted, he hung with a pretty nerdy, brainy crowd, so there probably wasn't much partying going on, but still). Even now, Zain has to do the reaching out to get his friends to come around.

It is lonely.

Recently, I was pondering the profound sense of not belonging that I grew up with. It occurred to me that I have given birth to a soul who epitomizes this struggle.

After Zain was born, long before I began officially studying to become a yoga teacher or the field of epigenetics, I heard myself say, "The long lineage of suffering and trauma in my family lives in and stops in Zain's body."

In an "Introduction to Ayurveda" workshop given by Rylee, she talked about the three doshas: vata, pitta, and kapha. According to Ayurvedic principles, we all have all three doshas, or energy patterns, but often, one or two are more dominant in our personalities.

Vata is represented by the elements of Space and Air, commonly equated with Spirit. When a vata-dominant personality is out of balance, this often leads to anxiety. His or her season is the fall, the cool, dry season characterized by death and grief. When vata is balanced, usually through exploration and curiosity about what is causing the anxiety, depression, or disquiet, the result is joy.

Because the nature of air is erratic, vata-dominant types tend to be really tall or short or not in the normal range physically or emotionally. Rylee says that vata types tend to be outliers and their role in this physical plane is to expand consciousness about what it means to be human.

And that, in a nutshell, is my son.

Recently, Zain found and contracted professional models to pose for him nude while he photographed them. He has a vision that is unique. I guess it's no surprise really. His vision *is* unique. He sees everything from the perspective of sitting in his chair. He has a different relationship with his body, his life, and his world than most people his (or any) age. What he then does with these images is breathtaking. Using photoshop to create a montage that incorporates Nature with parts of the body, he sees possibilities that far exceed anything my mind is capable of, possibilities that expand my view of what the world is and can be.

CB

The healing process is messy. The writing process is messy. Life is messy.

I remind myself of this when I get lost. This week, I got lost.

I knew that I would not be able to write, focus, listen, or hear the quiet voices of the inner world until Zain's wound was healed. And I was unsure it ever would.

This was very scary. The notion of this possibility consumed me. Every waking moment in the dark, it covered me, like a blanket too heavy for the season. I tossed and turned. I asked for help. Enlisted the same energetic forces that have been guiding my own healing to work— to work on my son.

Little Me got angry. She got very, very angry. Her clenched fists were raised, and she came out punching. Only, not at me. She came out punching at my husband.

My husband, one week away (and the most preoccupied he ever gets) from his own creative baby, the twenty-third annual New Directions Cello Festival—a feat of love of magnanimous proportions—was the target.

"I am so angry at you," I said at the breakfast table.

"I'm so angry at you," I said at lunch.

"I hate you right now," I said at dinner. Clearly, I had forgotten that this is a sign that Little Me needs some of my own attention.

I felt I was carrying the weight of Zain's newest health crisis alone. Well, not exactly alone. My therapist Joel showed me great kindness and support. My mother and Dappy were there on the ground. The women in my women's group listened softly when I told them of my worries. My friend, Mira, took me to Ithaca Sheepskin to get a medical grade sheepskin for Zain's bed. My yoga teacher, Demi, encouraged me to call in my own healing powers. My writing friend sent healing animal spirit love. Really, when I look at it, I was drowning in a sea of support. Why then, was it so important that I feel it from my husband?

It is Sunday, exactly five days from the first time I looked at Zain's sore. His aides have religiously applied the antibiotic cream to the afflicted area three times a day all week long. He has reduced his time in bed by two hours a day and spent at least an hour a day on one of his sides to get off the spot. Otherwise, it has been business as usual.

Only it hasn't been for me.

I spent the week tortured. Only the sight of my son, looking and acting healthy as usual, could calm the uncertainty that had pitched a tent in my belly. Even then, the worry just took a short nap before it came back even more flushed with life. Life has a way of showing us where our yoga practice needs to be strengthened!

Dappy and my mother have come to town. It is hot. Ninety-five degrees hot in early June. Fresh transplants are wilting in the garden from the heat.

Around 4:30 p.m., we all go over to Zain's house to have a look at his sore.

I am edgy. We move to Zain's room to examine him.

There is a shuffle to get Zain from his wheelchair to his bed. We place a sling behind his body and under his butt and legs. We move all the furniture out of the way to maneuver the Hoyer lift into position. A lift, a shift, and back down he goes. The hospital bed must be in just the correct upright position. Zain pushes buttons while his body magically lifts and lowers, and the head of the bed moves. Once he's down, the bed is readjusted again, he is turned with a sheet folded under his body for this purpose. Chris and I shift him back and forth as we shimmy his shorts down to expose his bottom. Dappy powers up a strong spotlight that I hold as we all take turns looking at the spot.

The stress in the room is palpable. I try hard to maintain my focus. To breathe while my mother tries hard to stay out of the way.

"It's gone!" I exclaim.

I can't believe it. I can see the bottom of the sore. There is no more pus, just a small indent at the bottom of his butt crack.

"It's healed," I say.

"See Mom? I told you that you didn't have to worry about it," Zain says to me still lying on his side.

"I need a drink," I say once we've got Zain dressed again and Chris is lowering him back into his wheelchair. I don't really want to drink; I want to cry. My body is rigid. It is not ready to let go of the strain of five days of incessant worry, constant conversation, planning, prayer, and oversight. It is not ready to be normal. Not yet. Not just yet.

Little Me is still angry. She has been neglected. Again. And she wants to fight.

ଓଃ

"Your mom really loves you," I say as I take Zain's stubbly chin in my hands. He knows I have been worried. I tell him about the prayers, about how I sent all my healers his way.

"Maybe you're the one who healed me," he says.

"Maybe," I say as I give him a kiss on the head.

Chris, my mother, and Dappy have already headed over to our house. I move the Hoyer lift out of Zain's bathroom so that he can pee. Help him change the memory card in his camera. Readjust his feet.

The heat outside has not abated. We move through it as one moves through a room with a furnace running full tilt.

"Why don't you let us take you out to eat," Dappy says earlier in the day as he lounges like a cat on our sofa.

"We already have all the food," I say, but I am tempted.

"That way, you don't have to cook in this heat."

"Yeah. Let someone else suffer so that we can eat."

I talk to Chris about it. He pushes strongly for staying home.

"We already thawed the meat. You bought the potatoes. We have wine. The back garden is beautiful and what about the new patio furniture?" he says.

I have lost the battle.

Now, in the kitchen, eggs and potatoes boiling for the potato salad, I start to feel resentful. My blood sugar level is low. I am shaky and still recovering from the stress of the week. My mother wants to be helpful. Our kitchen is the size of the galley of a small sailboat.

"We should have gone out to eat," I say to Chris, hissing from the side of my mouth.

I'm exhausted and the meal prep feels nearly impossible. We cook most nights, and I thoroughly enjoy it, rarely feeling stressed.

What is different tonight?

Besides the tremendous let down, relief, and emotional exhaustion of the past five days, this is the first time I've seen my mother since the fight on Mother's Day at her house. She has been lovely, supportive, and understanding of my state. She talks loudly. Lives loudly. But she doesn't ask for me to pull it all together. Her compassion is sincere. Still, there is an underlying current; a stress that pulsates beneath each moment.

I don't trust her. Can't look at her fully. Won't let her in. Her love touches my skin but does not penetrate.

"I can help you in the garden," she says.

We go out together. I pull back the row cover to expose mixed greens, spinach, lettuce, and arugula. I cut greens and fill the basket. I snap asparagus.

Inside, I assign her the task of cleaning the greens. We are not used to working together in my small kitchen. We navigate around each other awkwardly, trying not to step on a foot or cut off a finger. Zain and Dappy talk loudly in the living room about the artistic process, while Chris moves in and out of the kitchen, tending to the fire.

Little Me is raging. She is just under my skin and each moment threatens to flare.

"I need your help in here. Since when did fire tending take up all your time?" I ask Chris who is holding his phone to his ear talking to his grown son, Albert.

"Now is not the time," I say as I mix the Dijon mustard, rice wine vinegar, mayonnaise, and capers.

He hangs up and heads for the sink to rinse his hands.

"Could you prepare the asparagus for grilling?" I say.

"Oh, I can do it," says my mom. She is trying so hard to do everything right. I need her help, can't imagine getting dinner ready without her, and still, there is tension in my body with her near.

Once I finish preparing the potato salad, put it in the fridge, and make the salad dressing, I go out back alone to take a break.

I sit in one of our new patio chairs. I rock myself back and forth as I watch Chris's back. He is hunched over the grill twenty feet away, scraping and turning. He closes the cover and heads my way.

"I hate you right now," I say as he stops at the table on his way back into the house.

He looks at me gently and says, "I'm sorry you feel that way," before he continues on.

"This is why. You can't even stop for me. Not for a minute."

"I just put the buns on. I have to get the place settings inside," he says.

He stops, but I can see that he is already in the kitchen in his mind. He wills his body to stand still, while the rest of him keeps moving forward.

"Forget it. Just go."

And he does.

Finally, we eat. Everything is delicious. The birds move from branch to branch, call to us from up high. A frog croaks in the small fishpond.

"It's beautiful back here," my mother croons. "It is so nice of you to make this lovely meal for us."

"It almost killed me," I say as I look at her sideways.

"I know," she says and gives me a smile.

My blood sugar level slowly rises. I drink a few sips of Old Vine Zinfandel. Notice my lips are curving up into a smile here and there. Chris tries to take my hand, but I refuse it. I'm still mad at him.

"How many times a day do I tell you I hate you?" my mother asks Dappy.

He puts up one hand.

"How many times a day do you tell me you love me?" she asks.

He puts up two hands.

They laugh.

"I don't usually tell Chris I hate him. That happens just very rarely," I say.

"But you told me that today," he says in front of everyone.

"Yeah. Because in that moment, I did."

"What about now?"

"Oh, shut up."

We all laugh. My stress has begun to dissipate. Little Me has gone off to take a nap under a bleeding heart in the garden.

My mother takes my hand and starts to rub between my thumb and first finger. Instantly, I feel that familiar sensation. A subtle invasion. Her touch says too much. Asks for too much. I want to pull my hand away, but I don't. I let her hold it. Let her keep it. I know it is important for her to be able to touch me, just as it's important for me to be able to touch my son. I am aware of the odd quality of her touch. It doesn't quite feel maternal. I sit with it, notice the sensation. I listen to it all, the unheard words of the child that get stuck in my throat, the judge with a gavel, and the wise woman who sees.

⚃

Chris turns out the light in the kitchen to come join me on the couch after dinner. Everyone has gone. The house is quiet. The screen is set up for the nightly viewing of *Velvet*. We walk outside to see the moon.

"You are an excellent husband in so many ways," I say. "But emotionally . . ."

The moon is two days beyond full. The strawberry moon came out Friday. Enormous. Dramatic. Brilliant. It made its way up through sparse clouds reflecting the sun mysteriously into the night.

"He doesn't know much yet about water," Joel said to me in an early session when I was talking about my marriage.

Chris gets defensive, as usual.

"Just hear me," I say. And as I begin to tell him why today was so emotionally difficult, I realize that I am just hearing myself for the first time as well.

I am reminded once again, that I can't expect him to know what I need before I do.

"I needed to feel you with me today," I say. "It was the first time I was seeing my mom after the fight. We were finding out about Zain's pressure sore. I just needed to feel like you were there, knowing all that."

Little Me is talking. She is talking to Chris. She is talking to me.

We listen.

We hug.

I soften.

Chapter Ten

Belonging

Leaving my job, ending my career, and working full time on healing my body and mind are taking a toll. I see there is an "Energetic Hygiene" workshop being offered by Jasmina at Lakhi and sign up.

Seated in the big room, the workshop begins with us each creating a protective energetic bubble. We are given crayons to draw what we see during the energetic protection meditation. My picture is of a person standing inside a vibrant egg-shaped energetic field of yellow and orange. Each chakra is lit up, but there is constriction at the throat and solar plexus chakras. A large dark cloud hovers over the lungs and heart, and dark figures lurch out of my abdomen. Blue and green surround the pulsing energy field around my body.

We go outside for "plant limpia".

Jasmina, who owns a farm with her husband and young child, has brought cuttings of several medicinal plants from her land to the workshop: mugwort, rue, yarrow, lavender, calendula, and chamomile. The plants are laid out in piles on a blanket under the cover of shade. She invites each of us to make bouquets of the plants that she will then use to cleanse our energetic fields. Supposedly, the plants take on the negative energies we are carrying and leave us clean or *limpia* in Spanish.

When it is my turn, I give my bouquet to Jasmina, who adds more mugwort and yarrow to the mix before she begins working on me.

This should be good, I think, seeing the now enormous-looking bouquet in her hand.

Jasmina laughs.

"No worries. I got more plants for everyone. Now, your job is to breathe, relax, and let the healing in," she says as she starts to move the plants over my body.

The moment the plants touch my chest, a deep wail rises from my groin, up through the center of my body and exits my lips. My body convulses and sobs as I look on, surprised. I hadn't come to the workshop feeling sad or angry.

"That's it," Jasmina says softly as she touches my shoulder with her free hand. "Yes."

She speaks to me in a gentle maternal voice as my spirit splits open. I am having a hard time getting air, the sobs are coming so quickly. I am dizzy and my knees are weak.

"It's here, where you drew the cloud around your lungs," she says as she shakes the plants over my chest. "There is ancestral pain here that is not yours. You don't need to carry it any longer."

She begins to beat at my breasts with the bouquet.

"Is this okay?"

"Yes," I laugh between the tears streaming down my cheeks.

She slaps at my breasts and on my back between my shoulder blades. After several minutes, she slows down.

"You don't have to work so hard for love," she says. "Take this."

Jasmina hands me one of her "tools" as she calls them. Among the tools are rattles, feathers, gourds, small drums, rosewater, and sage that she invited us to use before our plant limpia to help dislodge stuck energy. She gives me a liquid she says jumped into her hand as she was collecting tools in the morning for the workshop.

"This is powerful medicine. It will close any lingering holes in your energy field. Rub some on your heart and your belly," she says. "You might want to lie down for a while."

Then she gives me a stalk of white yarrow.

"I want you to smell this. I want you to fill the space we cleared with positive energy and things that smell and feel good."

She pinches the yarrow flowers between her fingers and brings them to my nose. It has a pungent pleasant odor. I take hold of the plant and keep pinching the tiny buds close to my nostrils as I go inside to lie down.

Later, after all five participants have undergone the plant limpia process, we sit in a circle.

"Energy follows intention. Intention follows attention."

At the start of our workshop, before we visualized our protective cocoons of light, Jasmina spoke of the very first principle of protection.

"Before you can intend protection, you must first believe that you deserve good boundaries and protection. You must feel worthy of protection. That it's okay not to take into your body the pain and problems of others. You must feel that there is a part of you that gets to decide what comes in and what doesn't."

Ah hah.

Brené Brown, in her latest book, *Braving the Wilderness,* talks about how our worthiness and sense of belonging is nonnegotiable. "We carry it within ourselves," she says.

Do I?

For how long has my soul been carrying the pattern of not feeling worthy? Of love? Of protection? Of the right to decide what comes in and what doesn't? Of the right to belong. This old, negative ancestral pattern is shared by so many of us, but *particularly* by women whose bodies have historically not been respected, honored, or treated as their own.

In *Taking the Leap*, Pema Chödrön, suggests that our wounds may go beyond the hurts of this lifetime,

> . . . possibly ours is a far more ancient wound; perhaps we've been carrying these same tendencies, these same ways of reacting, from lifetime to lifetime, and they keep giving birth to the same dramas, the same predicaments.

Jasmina adds that it helps to have something physical that you carry or put on with the intention of protection.

I think of my long black corduroy Prince-style button up jacket. Each time I put it on I feel protected from life's assaults. Since getting back from the Yucatan, I have put it on any time I felt the need for an added dose of security out in the world. I have worn it pretty much every day until the temperatures rose and made wearing it uncomfortable.

"I like that coat," friends say when I have it on.

"Thanks," I reply running my hands down the front of the corduroy, grateful for the additional layer of safety it provides.

◌ß

I start this week's session with Joel in a tizzy. No one from school has reached out to see how I'm doing since I left.

"You really didn't get much support up there on the hill," Joel says. My hand moves to the pulling sensation in my spleen.

"There's a reason animals herd together. It's as old as time itself. A herd is protected from its predators. The bison that gets isolated from the herd will get eaten," he continues.

My hand moves from my spleen to my heart.

"There's a very real sense of not belonging that's happened here," he adds.

Tears slip out so fast I stop trying to wipe them away.

For some reason, I think of my mother.

"I don't think I liked being in my mother's body," I say after a few minutes of silence.

"You mean as a baby?"

"Yes. There was a lot of pain in that body."

I came into this world covered in the amniotic fluid of a traumatized body. Of a person who had not yet learned to belong to herself when I was born. I remember Jasmina's mantra, *I remove the swords that were placed upon me and lay them in the water.* I say it quietly to myself.

Joel's right fingers are tucked under his leg while his left traces a circular pattern on the end of the arm rest. I mention the work I'm doing with my inner child.

"I really think of the inner child as synonymous with vulnerability. And without this vulnerability, we can't truly know love," he says. "The two go together."

"What two?"

"Strength and vulnerability."

Something stabs my heart.

"I have never felt like I belonged anywhere," I say. Joel hands me two tissues that I use and ball up immediately.

"You belong here Marcy. It is your birthright."

His words touch the heart of my distrust.

"You belong just as you are. You needn't change a thing."

At the close of our session, I can't stop crying. My heart, burst wide open, feels the grief of years, maybe lifetimes, of not belonging.

"I want to acknowledge the fierce survivor in you, Marcy. You maintain even without the external structures to hold you. You always have."

He holds out his hands to me and I take them. We stand. We hug. I try to pull myself together, but I can't. I don't want to.

"Can I come back tomorrow?" I say, half-jokingly as we make our way down the narrow staircase.

These tears are cleansing me. Ancient me. Ancient all of us who have ever felt left behind or rejected by the herd. I am gently being called back to the herd of humanity, where I've always belonged. Perhaps even where I've always been.

The next day, I get sent out of the herd by Ida, my writing teacher.

ʘ

Ida enthusiastically welcomes me as I enter.

"Hello Marcy! Why don't you take this seat right here."

She motions to an uncomfortable-looking rocking chair with too many cushions. Today, there are only six chairs in the circle leaving large gaps of space that give the room an off-kilter feeling. As the students in the room titter about the strange feeling of the circle, Ida lets us know she is in no mood for jokes. She's in a bad mood and can't handle any comments about the circle. Moments later, she offers for a student to move her chair to make the circle more cohesive.

Once everyone has arrived, the clock strikes ten and we are settled. We sit for a few minutes of silence. Ida introduces the spark—a list of book titles, lines from song lyrics, or poetry—often depicting a theme. Each week, the theme changes.

In my writing groups, I try to write about something that is fresh; I strive to be open and honest and intentionally move toward, instead of away from, what is painful.

It's not for everybody.

Apparently, it isn't for Ida. Or, at least, not anymore.

She tells me so.

I come out of the bathroom after class to find Ida talking with Tom, a member of the circle. I hear him say how good it felt to write something vulnerable and share it with the group.

"Oh, I *never* do that!" she replies, emphatically waving a hand as though shooing away a fly.

When she sees me enter the room, her voice gets quiet as though she were saying something I shouldn't hear.

"Do I share too much?" I venture naively as I walk toward them. Ida turns her head toward me and says quite simply,

"Yes. Yes, you do."

The hair raises on the back of my neck. My body braces for the impact. She sends Tom away, turns to me and continues, "I wouldn't normally tell you this, but since you asked . . ."

It is clear she finally has permission to say something she's been wanting to say for a long time. I stand frozen while Ida unloads. My writing is simply too much for her. It makes her uncomfortable. It makes her feel things that she "didn't sign up for." It's too long. There's too much detail. It's too personal.

"You're writing about your son and your father and yourself . . ." Her voice trails off.

"I'm not sure what to do with what you're telling me," I answer, my neck and shoulders stiff as glaciers.

"Don't do anything. Or just sit with it. The last thing I would want is for you to write to please the teacher. That's a big no-no," she says.

I don't believe her. Can't conceive of a way to come back to class without this knowledge influencing what and how I write.

The only piece of writing I have written and shared in the group that I'm *sure* she likes since we started in early September is a piece called "Red Leather Bootstraps." While I wrote it, I was circling around something painful without fully landing or digging into it. Essentially, it was an avoidance piece; its style closer to something Ida might write.

I say so.

She agrees.

143

Here's what I hear Ida saying through my frozen filter:

"You're driving us crazy. Why can't you and your writing be lighter? Why can't it be more like mine? Or the others? You don't fit in."

A familiar pressure builds like a ripe fruit ready to burst through its skin.

 beta

Two orange-eyed tigers run through the bush on the cover of *Waking the Tiger, Healing Trauma* by Peter Levine. They remind me of the paintings of tigers on the walls of Joel's office.

Levine contends that trauma can be healed. His basic thesis is that we, like animals, experience trauma. Unlike animals, our trauma gets stuck in our bodies.

According to Levine, there are three basic parts to the human brain—the reptilian (instinctual), the limbic (emotional), and the highly evolved neocortex (rational). Reptiles have just the reptilian brain and function solely on instinct. A threat arrives. They fight, flee, or freeze. When the threat passes, they return to hunting for food, mating, or lazing on a rock. Their baseline physiology is quickly restored. Most animals have both the reptilian and the limbic brain. Threat comes. A herd animal moves closer to the herd. The herd usually flees together. When the threat is gone, prey animals will shake and tremble to release the stress, moving steadily back to a relaxed state.

Vulnerable creatures, the young, the wounded, or the old, will be those first preyed upon by the hunter. Just before being killed, the prey animal will freeze. This protects it from pain and potentially confuses the predator, who might think it is already dead.

Sometimes, when the animal pretends to be dead, it gets lucky and will be dragged to the tiger's den. Upon return to consciousness, it may escape, proceed to shake, tremble, shiver, and return to the fold of the herd.

Trauma, Levine writes, is physiological. A bird who flies into a window will shake off the trauma before it flies away. If this shaking is interrupted, it will go unconscious again. If interrupted too many times, it could very well die of fright.

Like the impala who freezes the moment it has been caught by the tiger, we often freeze the moment a trauma occurs. Story after story have been told of how a victim must be coerced to move away from the scene of the trauma. Children who have been kidnapped, hostages, women being raped; all will often stay unless pulled out. Why is this? Unlike the impala, we don't tend to simply shake off trauma once the threat to our lives has moved on. Our response gets complicated by the more complex workings of our brains. As a result, the energy gets trapped.

Trauma then sets up shop in the body. According to Levine, symptoms develop brought on by the "frozen residue of energy that has not been resolved and discharged." If we aren't able to complete the process of moving "in, through, and out of the 'immobility' or 'freezing' state," this residue gets stuck, causing havoc on the nervous system and in our minds and bodies. This can be seen in the "long-term, alarming, debilitating, and often bizarre symptoms of PTSD."

In his book, Levine tells the story of a group of children kidnapped from a school bus and shut up in a trailer dug into the ground. A later study of this group showed that the only child who didn't show signs of severe trauma in the following years was a fourteen-year-old boy who sprang to action to get everyone out when the roof of the trailer started to cave in. His ability to mobilize his fear and act during the traumatic event kept the energy from getting stuck in his body. Amped up emotions, like fear of bodily harm or death, flood the body in such moments. Most children, without the developmental skills necessary to respond, are met with an inability to act, stop, or influence the traumatic occurrence.

Levine works with his patients to reenact the heightened experience in the body at the moment of the original trauma. Since imagining the original trauma can be too triggering and cause the patient to reenter the mobilized state, the patient is asked to imagine something different that stimulates the same arousal. This allows the patient to act, experience mastery over, and move the energy that she couldn't at the time of the initial incident. At the precise moment when the patient embodies this mastery, Levine takes the patient back to the moment of original trauma and elicits the same active response.

Sometimes the healing takes place right then and there as the energy mobilized to fight the initial threat is finally successfully released. More often, it takes longer. The ultimate goal is to discharge this energy (like animals do) and restore it so that we may return to a "dynamic state of equilibrium."

I think back to my infant body suffused with fear, the strong instinctive urge to fight, and the impulse to flee. Without any of those possibilities at hand, the animal part of my brain surely took over and froze to protect itself.

The moment Ida turned toward me and told me stone-cold that I share too much in my writing, I froze. My body prepared itself, as it had learned to early on, for the devastating blow. My response to Ida was immediate, instinctual. The herd animal part of my brain stood before her, stiff and numb while she eviscerated me and my writing.

慘

Levine suggests that trauma sufferers get in the way of their own healing when they identify as survivors rather than beings with an "instinctual power to heal." Trauma is a natural part of life. No one can live life without experiencing some form of trauma. We would do well to follow the animal's model in rebounding from trauma. "We must pay attention to our animal nature to find the instinctive strategies needed to release us from trauma's debilitating effects," he says.

I move from Ida's house as though skating through a glacial tomb. Once in the safety of my car, the thaw begins. My mind shakes off the menace by firing rebuttals to every perilous word uttered by my teacher.

By the time I arrive home, I am dizzy from the swirl of defensive thoughts. I enter the house, take off my coat, hang up my purse, and lean against the door.

"Something happened today in writing class," I say to Chris who is preparing lunch in the kitchen. "I am going to need some time to be with it before I can talk about it."

"Okay honey," he says and walks over to give me a hug.

"I can't be touched right now," I say as I go upstairs.

Marcy, your writing sucks. You suck. Who do you think you are?

Worthlessness shrouds me, turns to heat. My clothes are on fire. I want to throw them off. Dive into the lake. Run to the next county to get away from the searing pain.

Instead, I stay. I don't abandon myself or the pain.

It hurts like a motherfucker.

Every time my rational mind jumps in to save me, it's quickly consumed by flames. Soon, I am ready to throw out everything I have *ever* written. Make a paper bonfire. Throw my computer into the inferno. Burn everything on my Google Drive.

As I approach total annihilation, I stay with myself. I move more fully into the unbearable.

"What you will discover is that it's just pain. And that pain is the other side of love. It was here before you got here. It is just something that is." Joel's voice echoes in my head.

After lunch, still embarrassed and ashamed, my mind says, "I have been an unwanted presence in the writing room, a scourge." But the instinct to heal has also been fed. My rational mind now has traction. I think of the work of Byron Katie. I ask myself what I *know* to be true.

All that I *really* know is that my writing stimulates something in Ida that makes her uncomfortable, something *she* doesn't want to feel. I remind myself of the many times fellow writers in the class have gone out of their way to appreciate my writing and tell me how my fearless and honest explorations have given them permission to do the same.

My prefrontal cortex works hard to inform my reptilian brain response, but a deeper, darker shadow still looms.

∽

In the morning, after a fitful-night of fighting demons, I awake heavy and dense.

As Chris and I get dressed, he makes sideways jokes that stab my aching body. He is oblivious to my immense suffering. He goes downstairs to make coffee while I sit on my meditation cushion to try to sort it out. I invite him to sit with me when he brings me coffee. I need him to know the pain I'm in. To not be alone. I need him to bear witness. I need him to hold this terrible hurt with me while I attempt to feel and release it.

As I speak, he does what he usually does, interrupts my flow to make comments and suggestions or to try to fix things.

"Stop," I say. "Please."

"You just need me to listen?"

"I just need you to listen."

He sits back. His face softens. I talk. I take my time. I stay in my body and gradually move closer and closer to the center of the pain. I am feeling feelings *I* don't want to: shame and worthlessness. I am grateful.

I continue to sit with myself, with Chris as my witness. When I hit dead center, when I don't shy away even a micromillimeter but instead melt completely into, *I am a worthless piece of shit with nothing to offer this world,* the miracle happens. The feeling moves left of center and floats off, weightless and empty. A clear blue sky is left with puffy clouds. Gentle rays of morning sun filter through the window.

Relief bordering on ecstasy.

I didn't die. Yes, it was painful, but those rugged, ugly feelings didn't kill me. I am cleansed, new, like the freshly wiped bottom of a baby.

Joel says there are about five general core issue patterns and *value* is one of them. Intimately linked to *belonging*, together, they may be my biggest triggers.

When Ida unscrupulously gutted my writing, she touched me there. Today, with Chris as my loving witness and support, I move toward this deep, overwhelming, and threatening sense of utter worthlessness, like a virgin sacrifice steps toward the edge of the volcano and jumps.

"Thank you," I say to Chris, my joy restored. We lean in to hug, and I am struck by how similar this process feels to the one I go through each time I seek to get physically intimate with my husband. Some part of me has to die in order to open fully to love, and that part fights the painful threat of its own annihilation every time.

∞

Each time I was unable to defend myself from abuse, each time those charged to protect me fell down on the job, the underlying unconscious message was *you are not worthy of protection.*

Pema Chödrön tells the story of a girl who dreams the same terrifying dream every night. Monsters chase her and chase her and she runs as fast as she can to get away from them.

"What if you got curious? Do you even know what the monsters look like?" She asks the girl one day.

The next time the girl has the dream, she turns to look at the monsters. The moment she turns to look right at them, they stop moving. They growl and scratch the air, but they don't take another step in her direction. She studies them. Gets to know them. Gradually, they stop growling and snarling and become quite benign. They never bother her again.

My sense of inherent value was taken as a young girl. Robbed. Stolen.

I cry, tremble, and shake, but do not die as I feared I might when this ominous feeling first threatened. This is the monster, the frozen energy unresolved after all these years. I release this untruth about myself as I let this intolerable feeling move through me.

I have faced the monster. I have experienced the pain of feeling complete worthlessness, and I have seen my inherent value. But there is something else. Something more.

That night, I wake in the dark. My body is covered in a thin film of perspiration. A feeling of dread comes over me as I recall, once again, my conversation with Ida. Suddenly, a "no" rises up from my belly. A fire. It burns the dread before it can take hold.

"No," it simply says. "You do not have the power to take away my value. You do not have the power to exclude me from the herd of humanity. You cannot tell me who I am. Only I can do that, and I choose to believe in my innate goodness, value, and right to be here."

I sit with the no. I sit in the no and know that I have found something. Something useful. A tool. A power. The next time I am triggered and sense the threat of annihilation where my instinct is to freeze, I can bring up this "no," from deep within and thaw it right then and there. This is the action that was missing so many years ago when I couldn't defend myself from the hurt to my body or the damage to my sense of value. This is the action I will call upon to protect me and my inner child from now on.

Unfortunately, I am not yet totally healed. The very next day I enter my morning yoga class at Lakhi once again wearing the cloak of unworthiness. No trigger. Just a dark shroud upon my person. The cloud covering the sky that is always blue. The lingering bruise from being hit.

Brené Brown says if you look for proof that you are worthless, you'll always find it. And it's true.

I see it, feel it everywhere. Even others' turned backs seem to be shouting, "You are shit!"

A friend's cursory hello at the start of class strengthens the case against me. I sit on my mat propped up by two folded blankets. My teacher Demi comes over, sits in front of me, looks me in the eye and asks, "How are you today?"

"Okay," I lie.

She keeps looking at me.

"Yeah," she says.

She lifts off my mat like a celestial bird and floats to her seat at the front of the room.

The dark cloud is still upon me. Can she see it?

I practice what I am learning with Joel and the Buddhist writings of Pema Chödrön. I stay with myself, shitty as it feels. I don't run or pretend. I just let the shitty feeling be present, as I start to move my body on the mat. I go inward, as far as I can.

Thank god for this practice of yoga. As I move my body and my mind toward a deeper state of alignment, it's impossible for this negative energy not to shift. By the end of the class, the shroud has lifted, the dark cloud moved on. I feel free once again; once again worthy of this life. The friend who I thought snubbed me, now comes over to chat.

"Now I can give you a proper hello," she says. "How are you doing?"

Has the shift in my mental space created the space necessary for her to come closer?

"I'm in the fire," I say. "I'm really cooking."

"Good. That sounds like a good place for you to be."

As we talk, I notice I have elevated myself. I am standing on two blankets while her feet are rooted firmly on the floor. I also notice a fearless authentic quality in my voice as I speak.

A poet friend of mine keeps a stool at the ready in her living room.

"When I speak, I prefer to stand on a soap box," she says one night when Chris and I have joined her and her husband for dinner. "It makes me feel powerful. We should all imagine we're standing on a stool when we have something to say."

Women.

In addition to our personal stories, which so often seek to confirm the false notion that we have no worth, we share the collective past of having our voices systematically ignored, devalued, interrupted, or stolen. It helps to have a soap box to speak from, even if it's imagined.

I walk slowly to my car after class. The sun is out. A soft breeze tickles the hairs in my nose. I marvel at the inner movement of the morning, that I could find myself in such a dark place an hour and a half ago and leave feeling full-hearted, beautiful, and free.

We possess the innate capacity to heal. I think. *Let it burn.*

Chapter Eleven

Lessons from Spain

It is the start of July, and we are on vacation in Spain. My ex-husband, Frédéric, has come to town to spend time with Zain so that Chris and I can get away. He is staying at our house (we have come a long way from the painful early days of our separation!).

Chris wanted to celebrate turning sixty this year with a three-week excursion to Spain where, at the age of twenty-five, he set out on his professional career in music. He and his late wife Cheryl came came here in the 1980s to spend a year. She would teach English; he would play his cello. They spent the next three years in Granada, where he made lifelong friendships with some of the best guitarists on the planet. Chris played himself silly, learned to speak Spanish with a lisp, and endeared himself to the local peoples.

Today, we find ourselves in Cádiz, a southwestern port city with a long history. Some say it is the oldest city in Europe. Founded by the Phoenicians, conquered by the Romans, then the Moors. Even Columbus loved this place. He set sail from its port twice for "the new world."

The streets are narrow with uneven cobblestone and filled with passing *ciclomotores* or mopeds. It seems like every member of the city has one and not one possesses a muffler. The sound of the motor explodes off the old city walls at all hours of the day and night, cutting through dreams and every passing thought. Walking the streets is a labyrinthian adventure, but every few yards, an oasis: another local *Cerveceria* or beer pub with tapas. No need to fret at any hour of the day that you will not be well fed. The seafood is abundant and reasonably priced.

Lunch starts at 2:00 p.m., dinner at 10:00 p.m. Families walk the streets with their toddlers until after midnight. Around 3:00 a.m., I can safely remove my earplugs to get sleep, though some folks work then as well. Last night around 4:00 a.m. a loud truck stopped in the street below while someone unloaded glass bottles. I fumbled for my earplugs.

I came here knowing it would disrupt my healing flow. I thought I could take a break. Fill up on Iberian pork and fried fish, walk long stretches of brown sandy beach, and marvel at the dark tans of the natives who never seem to tire of the relentless Atlantic sun.

No such thing.

Why am I suffering so much? I wonder.

My heart is on fire. Nothing feels right. After five days in this country, I haven't found a rhythm. My husband is distracted. When he isn't texting his Spanish musician friends to set up the next recording session, he is practicing what he will play behind closed doors. When he finishes, and we venture out into the city, I find him distant, still processing.

I am alone. Waiting. Wanting. Desperation begins to set in. I can feel depression at the edge of my psyche. I fight it. Fling insults at it.

"Come now," I yell at myself, "you are in Spain. Chin up. Look around. Life is happening everywhere."

But I am lost. In a sea of chubby Spaniards drinking *cervezitas* (tiny glasses of beer—ironic because the glasses don't seem so small to me). I can't find myself reflected in any face or locale. I am drowning, slowly. Painfully.

That night, I dream of my son. He is five years old and still walking. His face is cherub-like and he exudes peace and joy. I watch as he walks up the frame of a bicycle turned on its side. He falls on his head. When he gets up, he is still smiling, as though nothing has happened. He keeps moving, seemingly unaware of the pitfalls and dangers that await his unstable body at every turn.

The next day, walking through the old city, we pass an advertisement in a store window. It is of a mother and son. The boy in the poster reminds me of my dream. A strong pulse hits my heart. The hot sun hits my head. I stumble on the uneven surface of the cobblestone. We keep walking.

We arrive at the beach around 6:00 p.m. The sun is still high in the sky. There are umbrellas and tan, greasy bodies everywhere. We find a spot in the scorching sand toward the edge of the people line. The walk has taken over forty-five minutes. We are boiling and tired and in need of a swim.

Still, I am lonely.

"I'm all yours," Chris said as we began the long walk through the city toward the beach. Though our bodies walked closely, I felt invisible, the silence between us broken only by the loud interruption of the constant stream of mopeds speeding by.

Now at the beach, we set up our umbrella, our blanket, and our towels. Chris is already weaving his way toward the water through the diverse sea of figures in beach chairs while I watch. How long will it take for him to realize I am not at his side? Halfway to the water's edge, he stops and turns around. But it's already too late.

"I am all yours," he had said, but he didn't even notice I wasn't walking with him.

I look at him from the small, temporary home we have erected. *I am suffering.* My suffering is so strong I think it will swallow me. I walk to the water in the opposite direction. I avoid Chris. I want to hurt him the way I am hurting.

I am invisible. No one sees me. The waves hit my body. My bikini top comes undone. Chris, now at my side, ties it for me. We argue. I wonder if the next wave will pull me out to sea.

I leave the water alone.

Back on the blanket, I try to tell Chris what I am feeling. *But what am I feeling? Do I even know?*

I blame him for my sadness. My grief. My hurt. He is defensive. Says that maybe I'm just an unhappy person. Then takes it back. We fumble. I need him to caress my heart. My soul. He doesn't know how. I leave. Take off down the beach. Walk away. Let my legs move me away from what I think is the source of my suffering.

I recite the mantra I learned last summer with Tempa Lama. I say it again and again as I kick up the water with my toes. One foot in front of the other. One foot in front of the other. Perspective. I am seeking perspective. I have gotten lost in the smallest miasma of myself. A bitter hole. A downward spiral that suffocates. Where the air is heavy and stagnant and dead.

Still invisible, I observe my surroundings as I walk. Young children play in the waves. Fathers teach their sons how to swim. Teenagers and twenty-somethings hit small balls back and forth with wooden paddles. Young men with taut muscular bodies kick the soccer ball back and forth. Grandmothers hold the hands of babies learning to walk, their toes in the water. Bellies roll as men and women kick back in low beach chairs smoking cigarettes; voices hoarse as they laugh. Women gather in groups knee deep in gossip, breasts covered and exposed.

I walk on, invisible.

Finally, I turn around and the sun hits my face. I take off my sun hat. Take in the view of the Cádiz cathedral miles down the beach shrouded in a fine mist. I am still reciting my mantra as

I head into the waves to swim. A large wave knocks me down and takes my hat.

"Infinite respect," I say to the ocean and bow. I retrieve my soaked hat from the next wave.

Halfway back, the opening comes. My longtime practice of bodhicitta, or awakened heart, rises to the murky surface. The mantra designed to remove the obstacles that obscure Pure Consciousness is working.

We are all suffering; I think as I look at two young girls making a small moat with their feet in the sand. *This very human feeling of being invisible, unseen, and unknown. Every person on this beach has or will feel this way at some point in his or her life.* And just like that, I am home again. I have reentered the sea of humanity. I float with every scantily dressed being whose path I cross. An abundance fills me, and I am one with everything.

I keep reciting my mantra. I let love fill every pore of my skin. I radiate it back as I drink in the gentle rays of the late-day sun. Feeling the warm sand under my feet, I commune silently with every vulnerable heart I cross on the beach.

Then I see him. In his long red bathing trunks. Making his way through the active bodies all around. He sees me. Walks straight toward me with a smile on his lips and in his eyes. But I am not ready. He tries to touch me, I say no. We walk back together, but I am careful. I have just rediscovered a fragile moment of peace and contentment.

We swim. Together and apart. The parallel play of children. Chris wants to get close. I am not ready.

We argue again back on our towels, him in the shade of the umbrella, me in the sun.

"I'm trying," he says. "I'm doing everything I can."

"You're not or else I wouldn't be feeling this way," I say, still falling into the old pattern of blaming him for my pain.

We lie down. My jaw is tight. My heart pinched and protected. After what feels like hours, Chris touches the soft skin of my forearm. He caresses it gently. Lovingly. I turn toward him on my side. My eyes are closed. I am crying. I let all the sadness, pain, and grief show on my face. He sees me. He is soft.

"That dream about Zain really affected me," I say quietly, eyes closed. "He was walking on such unstable ground. He kept falling, but then he would just get up and do it again. He wasn't learning from his mistakes."

My voice trails off and the sobs begin. Small at first, then like waves growing larger as the weather shifts and the wind kicks up. I let them come and realize I am not only crying for my son; I am crying for myself.

I have been reenacting a childhood story. I see myself at five years old, alone with an earache crying in pain, knowing my mother won't come because she is out. Even if she were home would she see me? It is nighttime and my father has fallen asleep in his armchair with a cigarette burning between his fingers. I don't dare wake him. Back in my bedroom, I sit on my bed, looking out into the night. Alone. Suffering. In pain waiting to be rescued. But the rescue never comes. I cry myself to sleep.

I learned to harden my heart early on, like so many who adapt to escape the unbearable pain of loneliness. Here, on vacation in Spain, I have done it again.

As the grief leaves my body, I remember.

"Little Me!"

She has been large and in charge and beating me (and everything within arm's reach) senseless until I wake up and take note. She is my work now. My raison d'être.

I thought I could go on vacation. Take a break. That she would be okay for a little while back in Ithaca, while I went to Spain.

Wrong.

She is awake and she is pissed.

"Okay, Little Me" I say. "I got the message. I can't just abandon you. I can't just leave you behind."

Chris comes close, kisses away my tears. I am spent. All defenses washed to sea in the ocean of humanity's salty tears.

We hug and lie quietly. My body is marshmallow. While I am grateful for the softening, I wonder how long it will take for me to learn that *I don't need to work so hard for love.* How long before I equate the inner child with vulnerability.

"I think Zain is my teacher," I say.

My friend warned me earlier, that Zain was trying to come into my writing.

"Pay attention to when he comes in," she said.

"Maybe he is reminding you to soften," Chris says.

ଔ

In one of my last therapy sessions before our trip, I talk about Zain.

"I can't protect him," I say. I see my son's body slowly unravel as time marches on.

"No. You can't."

Pema Chödrön warns in *The Places That Scare You* that the way of bodhicitta is never knowing what will happen to us next.

We can try to control the uncontrollable by looking for safety and predictability . . . but the truth is that we can never avoid uncertainty.

Is this what Zain is trying to show me in my dream? That there is no such thing as a stable surface to walk on? For any of us? Is that why he keeps smiling even after he falls, because he's already got this figured out?

In *El Zahir*, by Paolo Coelho, the protagonist goes on a spiritual journey. His beloved wife has left him without a word or a trace. He walks the Camino de Santiago de Compostela in northern Spain to try to understand what has happened and proceeds to write a novel in the book called *Tiempo de Romper, Tiempo de Coser* or *Time to Come Apart, Time to Come Back Together*. He comes to think of his missing wife as "El Zahir," or "an obsession." His obsession is to understand why she has left and get her back.

A young man named Mikael shows up who knows the wife. He even knows where she is. After two years of missing his wife, the protagonist (whose name is never mentioned in the book) wants one thing: To be with her again. Mikael, who has a very special spiritual gift, helps him, not to find his wife, but to find himself, something he must do if he is ever to see her again.

And thus, begins this character's personal journey to liberation. What is he moving toward?

What are any of us moving toward?

Love.

In Coelho's novel, the main character learns about the universal principle of Love. Mikael, who has been sent to spread this knowing throughout humanity, teaches him to let go of his personal story little by little in order to know the abundance of his truest nature, Love. The main character reaches for a book on his bookshelf and without looking, opens to a page that talks about the *punto acomodor* or turning point. In our lives, there is always a turning point, a moment, an event, or an experience that is responsible for the fact that we have stopped growing. It could be a trauma, an intense disappointment in love, or even an overwhelmingly positive experience we don't yet know how to integrate. According to this book, if we want to keep growing, free ourselves to live our truest nature more fully, we must go back, remember, discover, heal, and, ultimately, retrieve what got lost at this turning point.

Ω

On Friday, we spend the day in Tangier, winding the narrow streets of the Medina and Kasbah. First and final stop: a rug store. We are completely seduced by the talented salesmen in the rug Bazar, and after several cups of steaming hot mint tea, much haggling, and comments such as "Happy wife, happy life," we leave with a beautiful silk rug. Mid-sales pitch, the salesman almost makes an irreparable gaff.

"In our country," he says, "we think of the man as the head and the woman as the neck. You can't have a head without a neck, so you need to treat your wife well." *I am nobody's neck,* I think as I continue to smile pleasantly. Then my bare foot touches the silk carpet and I am swept away.

We board the ferry back to Tarifa, and before it has left the port, I am asleep, head turned toward the window, mouth wide-open. Chris has gone off to get himself a cold beer.

We arrive back in Tarifa, Spain, at 6:00 p.m. with an hour-long drive ahead of us to get back to Cádiz. The first port restaurant we see appeals to my hunger. I order *chipirones a la plancha* or grilled small squid. Eight perfectly grilled squid arrive twenty minutes later on a bed of lettuce with a few under ripe tomatoes and two lemon wedges. Inside each *chipiron* is a soft, white substance that I find repugnant.

"¿Se puede comer?" I ask the waiter.

"Claro. Es muy rico."

I eat it. It *is* delicious, but still a bit *asqueroso* (disgusting) in texture. By squid six, I can't take it anymore. I feel like I will throw up. I gently gift the remaining squids to Chris, who happily gobbles them up. As we walk the crowded streets of Tarifa back to where we parked the car, my stomach begins to rebel.

I order an ice cream. I think it will calm my stomach. And it does. For the entire time my tongue comes into contact with that delicious tiny ball of chocolatey Rochelle Ferro-flavored creamy gelato.

And then, the ache comes back.

"I'm worried about this ache in my tummy. I think something might be wrong," I say to Chris once we are on the road.

"When did it start?"

"After I did that 'Healing the Inner Child and Shamanic Journeying Workshop.'"

Since mid-May, I have had an on-again, off-again stomachache. It's not a stomachache in the traditional sense—although, never having had many stomachaches, I'm not even sure what that means. It's more like a dull pain just below the ribs where my stomach and gallbladder and pancreas live.

"I hope I don't have cancer," I suggest, as we make our way back west in the dark through a field of air turbines.

"Oh honey. You don't have cancer . . ." Chris's voice trails off into the night.

I try closing my eyes, but I can't sleep.

The next morning, I get my period and have my first bout of diarrhea.

"I feel like shit," I say as we begin packing up our things. "No pun intended."

I am totally out of sorts and am practicing mindfulness like crazy. It's hard to be mindful of your own misery, but I try my best.

The night before we went to Tangier, we dined with Chris's long-time musician friend, Javi, sixty-four, and his Venezuelan girlfriend Gabriela, thirty-eight, and had an amazing time. "I can't believe your

Spanish," they exclaimed as I looked at them sheepish and shy over the breadsticks.

"No me siento muy bien," I say today as Javi lets us in. *(I'm not feeling so well)*. I explain about the *chipirones* and my sensitive stomach. Aware of Javi's sensitive nature, I even tell him I've just started my period. For the rest of the day, he is very attentive to my every move. At the restaurant *Bar Santa María* in the old part of the city, he picks up the plate of fresh tomatoes and potato salad and holds it up while I serve myself an infinitesimal amount. I don't want to be rude.

"You need more care today because you're not feeling well," he says. I withhold a tear. I look over at Chris who isn't the least bit preoccupied by how crappy I'm feeling. A plate of Iberian ham, grilled red tuna, and four perfectly grilled steaks of croaker arrive. I eat sparingly.

My stomach has taken me to hell.

All throughout today's extravagant lunch, generously offered to us by Javi, I struggle. Unable to find my shine, my mind is under water, trapped in the downward movement of my intestines and uterus. The straight back of the chair pinches at my spine. I can't cross my legs under the low wooden table. I come in and out of the conversation.

Mindfulness, Marcy, I keep reminding myself as I try to sit up straighter. I breathe in. I breathe out. I listen and then I am submerged once again. Cross table conversation is too arduous a task at the moment. I'm letting everyone down. I'm a boob. I attempt to initiate conversation with Gabriela sitting to my right. She is her same energetic, smiling, bubbly self. I can see why Javi is in love with her. Her low guttural laughs. The way her bottom shakes when she walks. The sparkle in her eye.

We talk about her work. She is studying some form of body-focused psychotherapy in Madrid. We have much in common.

As we walk out of the air-conditioned restaurant, I whisper to Chris that I'm mad at him. All day long, even when I have stated it plainly, as in "my stomach is really hurting," my pain has been invisible to him. *How is it that my husband's friend is more attentive to my suffering than he is?*

"Oh honey," he says uncomfortably as we walk toward Javi's car after lunch in the scorching heat of the day.

Chris tries to comfort me by putting his arm over my shoulder. I shrug him off. In the backseat of the car, I shun every one of his advances.

When we get back, Javi and Gabriela scurry through the apartment filling their already packed bags with toothpaste and toothbrush before leaving for the next week. Finally alone in the apartment, sitting on the couch in the main room, Chris says, "I'm sorry honey. You know how I get. The curtains are closed and the air conditioning is running full tilt.

Chris is a middle child. He is constantly preoccupied with everyone else's well-being. At home, we can be in the middle of a deep emotional exchange and he will get up abruptly to leave.

"Where are you going?"

"To do the dishes at the Common House. I don't want to be late."

"Honey, they won't miss you for a few more minutes while we finish this conversation."

So, it's not a surprise that being with an old friend in a foreign country has him distracted. Still, it feels like shit.

My intestines roil as we make our way to a local beach. Floating in the sea water helps calm them. We return by walking shoulder deep in the warm soothing waters. Everything in me relaxes in the gentle rocking of the sea.

That night, in Javi's quiet, dark, air-conditioned bedroom, I get my first good sleep since we arrived in Spain. In the morning, I am still in a bad mood.

"I'm still mad at you," I say to Chris as we turn toward each other in bed.

"Why?"

"I don't know. I guess I'm blaming you for my suffering again."

"That's not fair."

"I know."

In my morning meditation, I explore this lingering feeling of anger. I tip it on its side and see that it has no roots, no underbelly. It is a mirage. A false story. An attachment to something that does not exist. That is not real.

Chris is *not* responsible for how I feel. I free him (at least for the moment) from this tangled web. I watch it float away and feel the freedom beyond its grasp. Energy starts to circulate through my systems once more. Again, I am reminded that it's *my* job to accompany myself. First. Before asking, or in my case, expecting, care from other. Even when I'm suffering.

When I finish my practice, I walk from the terrace through the opened doors of the bedroom. The morning air lifts the long, light, white gauze curtains.

"What do you want for breakfast?" Chris asks before he has even looked up from his phone to see my face.

I stop at the doorway to the room where he lies naked on the bed, cell phone in hand. I stand and wait for his eyes to follow his words. Chris puts his phone down and watches me as I walk to the window, look out at the asphalt covered streets, and feel the sun start to warm the day. Once I feel he's with me, I reply.

"Mushroom omelet."

We move together to the kitchen to make breakfast.

ℭℬ

While I know it's ultimately my job to accompany myself, I am not 100 percent sold on the notion that Chris doesn't share some responsibility for how I feel.

I ask myself the following questions:

What are we here for? Are we not also here for each other? Why stay in a relationship otherwise? For security? For food, clothing, and shelter? To have someone to go to the movies with. Someone to interrupt as they read the Magazine section of the Sunday NYTimes. Someone to turn to in the wee hours of the night for a snuggle when you can't sleep. Someone to satisfy carnal desire or simply so as to not feel so alone.

Well, yes.

And no.

Can we even do the deep healing work we need to do without a partner?

Can I?

Our first hurts, our first rejections, the first sense that there is something fundamentally wrong with us, often come from our first relationships.

There is no doubt in my mind that Chris came into my life as a force for healing. At the time of our wedding, I was under the false impression that the only one who had healing to do in the relationship was me. In my mind, Chris's spotless (my projection) upbringing meant that he was one of the few people on the planet who got the golden ticket to the theater marked "healthy childhood."

We wrote this spiritual intention into our wedding vows. "We come together to heal. To help each other move more deeply in the direction of truth and wholeness."

The next day, my stomach is calm again. I have found a secluded spot on the beach in El Palmar, one of the nicest beaches on the coast of Spain. Today, the beach is sparsely populated and stunning. The

Levante, a wind that comes in from Africa, is blowing from the East. The few families, friends, and couples who have dared come to the beach in these winds are huddled in front of El Gurúja, a small Spanish beach-style bar/restaurant, while I attempt to go it alone up the beach 100 feet. They clearly know something I'm about to discover.

Loose dry sand moves over the top of the beach caught up in this constant wind. It pelts my wet body as I make my way back to my towel after a swim. It enters through the miniscule holes of the zipper of my backpack sitting innocently under the umbrella I set up as a wind block.

I walk down the beach, explore the shelter provided by El Gurúja. My body, previously assailed by flying sand, likes it better here. With my towel now, just a few meters down in front of the restaurant, I have a good view of the goings-on. The loud music and constant flow of people in and out of the bar distracts me, but at least sand isn't entering every orifice of my body from the air. Sometimes we need to give up one comfort to have another.

Chris spends the whole day a few blocks away up the sandy road recording with his guitarist friend, Tabor. It is almost 8:00 p.m. and the sun is beginning to lower in the sky. Children are strolling by, throwing footballs, and shooting at each other with sticks they have found on the beach.

"What's up?" I text.

"Just finishing. What shall we do?"

"Come join me on the beach. I'm down in front of El Gurúja."

"K."

Fifteen minutes later, Chris is walking toward me in his red swim trunks, freckled white torso, tan neck and arms, long thin legs.

We open the blanket out to accommodate us both. He sits, but I can see he is still in the recording studio.

"I'd like to go for a swim. Wanna join?"

"No. I've already swam a lot today. You go."

While Chris swims, a small auburn-colored dog walks up the beach toward my blanket. I put out my hand for it to come over. It does. It is limping, not using its front right paw to walk on. It stops in front of me on the blanket. I pet it behind the ears and pause my hand on its back. Its breathing is labored. It is hard work to move through the thick sand as a short dog with only three good legs.

Where's your master? I inquire mentally. The dog looks around, then walks up toward the bar. I watch him, now worried that he has been abandoned. Two small dogs start to bark at him. I see that his tail is wagging and am surprised. He doesn't get mad at being barked at. Instead, he wants to be friends. Then, he makes his way through the crowd into the bar where I can no longer see him. Meanwhile, I've hatched a plan to bring him back to the States when we leave.

This is how people become dog owners, I think. *A dog shows up in need and chooses you.*

Chris is back. He shakes his wet head onto the blanket. It's been a long day for both of us. Him in the recording studio, me at the beach. I'm happy to see him but know that it will take a bit to find the sweet spot where we can connect. Chris seems unaware that there is some work to be done before we find our way back to each other.

Suddenly, I see the people who have been around me all day for the first time. *What has prevented me from seeing all these people today?* I wonder. *Really seeing them.*

The response is instantaneous.

Fear.

I turn and watch the people sitting at the various tables in front of the bar, having a *copa*, talking animatedly, smoking hand-rolled cigarettes. Large groups, small groups. Women with young children.

Fathers with young children. Several dogs sit next to a sign that reads, "No dogs."

It's not easy being alone as a woman all day on a beach.

In addition to that *off* feeling you sometimes get when you're in a new place and aren't sure you're truly safe—a feeling all too common to me as a woman—I realize I've been caught up in body all day. Not having a body. *Being* a body. The subconscious feeling of eyes evaluating my size and shape. The curve of my hips. The sway of my breasts as I walk. The sense that we're all checking each other out, comparing ourselves. Self-merit meted out in our body being *too much this* or *not enough that.*

While I might have enjoyed this in another context, I become aware of this feeling of being an object. To myself and to others. Caught up in this shallow universe that sees the self exclusively as physical body, I missed *being* myself all day long.

When Chris arrives, suddenly, I can relax.

Seven kids have begun to play right above our heads in the sand. I look up and see that a man at the bar has been watching us. The small auburn-colored dog with the limp reappears from the crowd. He begins to walk toward us but gets stopped by the loving hands of man with a goatee wearing a hat. He must be the bar owner.

Looks like he's in good hands, I think.

And so am I. Chris's and mine . . .

Chapter Twelve

Love Dance

Back from the sweltering heat of southern Spain, we return home to daily life and our untended garden. The basil is past its prime. As I walk into the house, arms bundled in pulled basil plants, I bump into Chris. He looks good to me. Not "oh, you're such a sweet man," good. *Edible* good. *Delicious* good. He is wearing a blue-and-white checkered cotton shirt, sleeves rolled up to the crease where upper arm and forearm meet. His worn, loosely belted Levi's jeans hang at his hips. The shirt billows out slightly just above his small buttocks. Chris is tall and lean, and no matter what position he takes, I just can't get over how appealing he is to me.

"I want you," I say as we kiss.

"We can go upstairs right now," he says, as he grabs my hand.

It is 5:42 p.m. I have just gotten home after another three-day intensive Anusara Yoga Teacher Training. Chris is just arriving home from an Ithaca College cello recital.

We kiss long and deep. My right hand instinctively moves to hold Chris's butt cheek. I pull him toward me. Our lips hold each other for a long time as we breathe in each other's essence. A holy moment. Just one more beautiful moment in a day already brimming with yoga weekend love.

Why do I choose not to run up the stairs and throw myself into my lover's arms right then and there, as he offers?

Because . . . Because it's 5:42 p.m. Because dinner needs to be made. Because I haven't spent any time outdoors all weekend and the late-day sun is shining. Beckoning. Because a short walk is in order. Because the basil needs to be processed. Because the peaches are beginning to spoil in the bottom drawer of the fridge. Because Zain is surely hungry, and so am I—the first signs of low blood sugar are creeping in, soon to make me very bad company.

I smile, consider the romp that might ensue if I were to surrender to the moment, and let go of my husband's hand.

We venture out onto the land. I slide my arm around Chris's waist as he lifts his over my shoulder. We are in perfect sync as we make our way across the pavement toward the grass. I imagine our next-door neighbor looking out as we pass.

Aren't we beautiful? I think as the sun hits my face and my hand is warmed by the firm flesh of Chris's right side.

And we are.

So why don't I drop everything, run up the stairs, and strip naked while I rip Chris's clothes off his body and jump his bones?

The truth?

The god-honest, raw, hold-nothing-back truth?

I am scared. Scared of so many things. Scared that once we get there, the entry into each other's deepest places will be rocky and obscure. Scared that we will end up needing hours instead of minutes to find delight. Scared that the bright light I have cultivated all weekend in my yoga training will somehow be diminished in the unrealized quest for perfect union with my man. Scared that the feeling of desire and delight I am sensing at first blush won't be strong enough to hold a transition to upstairs or an awkward groping for mutual pleasure. Above all, while it is what I wish for the most, I am scared of surrender. Of the inevitable death of ego necessary to succumb fully to love.

I envision a long, drawn out tomorrow instead. An alternative to dropping everything now, in this tight window before us. I visualize a rich Monday morning yoga and meditation practice followed by brunch and two luxurious hours in bed. I see us breathing together to align, then kiss, touch, explore, cry, talk, and move through the inner barriers standing in the way of total nakedness.

"What's your day like tomorrow?" I ask after dinner as we pluck the green leaves off the hardened basil stalks to be made into pesto.

"Well, I have a lesson at 10:45 a.m., and then an ISP meeting for Lillian at noon. I teach downtown at 3:00 p.m."

My heart sinks into my hot belly as my plan for Monday burns. What will I do with this desire? This deep longing for connection? This need to have my man all to myself for as long as it will take to get *there*? And, whenever *I* want him, no matter what *his* plans are.

I clip another tender branch from the hard core of the basil plant. My own core, once tender, vulnerable, open, and wanting, begins to harden as the core of the sun-loving basil plant hardens in the growing cold of autumn.

"Oh," I say. "That sucks."

We keep pulling basil leaves, careful to discard any that have begun to turn brown. A fuzzy white caterpillar clings to the underside of a branch.

"I was thinking maybe we could spend some time together tomorrow since we haven't really seen each other all week or weekend."

"We could make love tonight," he says.

"Yeah, but now I'm turned off."

"What do you mean?"

Fear has crept into my belly.

"I'm feeling bummed out and disappointed about tomorrow."

"Weren't you planning on writing tomorrow anyway?"

"Yeah. But I was willing to make an exception."

Fear tugs low in my belly. It is the fear that is almost always present when Chris and I turn toward each other to share ourselves deeply in the flesh. It is a dark shadow. A presence that emerges just when I don't want it to. A curse. The dark mark of history at the base of my spine.

I struggle with it. Fight against it. Cuss, kick, and scratch. I talk to it. Acknowledge its presence, but always, almost always, my fear emerges from the shadows just as I want to surrender my body, mind, and heart to union with my beloved.

I am embarrassed. I stand at the sink as I cut another branch, forage the stem for green leaves, and throw them one by one into the cold water. Why do I have to be so broken? Why can't I be like so many women in the movies, who move seamlessly from the first kiss to copulation leaving a line of discarded clothing all the way up the stairs? Why can't we kiss, steam up the windows with our passion, be a straight arrow toward orgasmic union? Isn't this what everyone else is doing?

Is it?

While I have learned to distrust the overt and covert messages drilled into us by all forms of media, this one always leaves me disturbed. Over and over, I see the same linear advance between a man and a woman toward coition. Rarely is that trajectory interrupted by cunnilingus, a flashback, stopping to talk, check in, breathe, cry, or laugh. Rarely do the two people seem lost or unsure what to do next. Woman on top. Man on top. Penetration. Sweat. Orgasm. And then it's done.

Bombarded by these media messages, I stand with my aloneness. Alienated. Rarely, if ever, do I find my story mirrored in the media. Am I a freak of nature? An anomaly? An abomination? A cosmic joke? I carry the disappointment of what I have always considered my sexual aberration like a shroud. An umbrella in the inky darkness of rain as I walk steadily toward my own tombstone.

The scars that linger and never fully heal.

How many other women are like me? How many other women need a different path into lovemaking and physical intimacy? How many other women need to breathe together with their partner? Look deeply into each other's eyes? Confront fear and shame and resistance to letting go, to letting the other in, to being seen and known deeply? To being so completely exposed?

How many other women need time to fight, to buck, to push love away, to go to the depths of their own ugliness, to see their lover's ugliness, to make their lover as ugly as they feel, before being able to take them fully into their hearts? Before entering the beauty and the bliss and the tranquility that awaits? The calm after the storm. The empty fullness. The fullness that never lasts long enough. The hard-won ease that erodes gradually, like exposed earth to drops of rain. The erosion of union that comes with every incoming text, email, and phone call following sex?

When I make love with Chris, it is like willingly entering a tropical storm. Gail force winds. Destruction. Death. Deconstruction. Of the self. A necessary process of giving over the smaller self to something much greater. It is a ripping away of all the mighty fibers of ego that edify and protect and define the self.

It is like volunteering to stand in front of the firing squad.

The French call sex *la petite mort*, or little death. Who would knowingly go to his or her own death without a fight? Even if that person knew that what awaits him or her on the other side is pure bliss? Who would voluntarily go through the eyewall of such an unrelenting storm?

"We could make love tonight," he says, so innocently, as if it were as easy as pulling basil leaves from the stem.

ℭℨ

The very next day, I want my husband and I do not hold back. My fear has left me through my writing. It is nowhere to be found.

We are sitting out back, under the faded red umbrella. We have eaten lunch. The honeybees move drunkenly from one white clematis flower to another. Occasionally, a newly hatched Monarch butterfly makes its way erratically over the hedgerow. The sound of a saw moves lazily around the side of the house. If we were smokers, we'd be puffing on a cigarette. Instead, we each sit back in our chairs and look at each other.

"I was thinking maybe we could go upstairs and make love," he says.

I look straight at him.

"But we don't have to," he says quickly, misreading my face.

"Could we just stay present with what you suggested?" I ask.

He moves closer to my chair. My eyes are drawn to the faint bulge next to his fly. I reach out and touch it.

"Don't move," I say.

I look into his eyes and feel my desire. Raging and thick. I move into it, feed it a log. Focus my energy into my belly. It burns. Ardent. Chris feels it, too. We go upstairs.

I undress him. I touch him. Taste him. Touch him some more. I stay in my fire. I want to be consumed by it. Consumed, period. Each time Chris reaches out to touch me, I push his hand away. Touching him is what I want. I take it. I take him. And then he takes me.

"It was new," I tell Joel in our next session. "Different."

I try to describe the energy I felt. The focus. The desire.

"I want this for myself," I say.

"You could just stay with the first three words," he suggests.

"I want this," I repeat.

I want this.

I don't stop wanting this.

The next day, I want this, but there is no time. So secretly, I burn. Chris can't see it. Doesn't detect it and, somehow, I am hurt by it. *Why can't he see that I want him?* I think of the rose in *Le Petit Prince*. The relationship of the little prince to the rose is an allegory for the complexity of the mind, heart, and soul of a woman. The prickly rose pushes the prince away when what she really wants is to be close. But she needs the prince to see her. Perceive her want even when she can't give herself permission to have it, share it, want it herself. I act like the rose that night.

"What are you doing?" I ask Chris.

We are both seated on our brown plush couch tapping away at our computers. Chris drums away at the keys one index finger at a time. His breathing seems shallow, and I can tell he is perturbed.

"What difference does it make?" he asks annoyed.

I go upstairs to shower. I come down naked with a towel on my head to peer at him from the middle floor mezzanine. He can tell his curt response hurt me and apologizes.

"I was trying to do something on the community boat calendar. I couldn't figure it out. I was just exasperated," he says.

I'm not ready to forgive him.

"Well, I'm still feeling hurt and rejected. I'm going up to bed to read now."

"I can come."

"Not yet. I need some time alone."

I don't read. I lay back on my pillows with the light on and breathe. Gradually, sleep falls over me. I am drifting off when I hear Chris start to move around downstairs. I quickly turn off the light. He sees the light is off and doesn't come up. He sleeps in Lillian's old room instead.

I am awake now. For hours. Wishing he was by my side. But, like the rose, too proud to admit it to Chris, I keep my desire secret. It is a long lonely night. And I want him. I want him all night.

CR

Later, before the sun rises, Chris crawls under the covers. I turn and my hand lands on his pubic hair. I can see the orange tint of the curls in my mind. I stroke it. Play with it. Then with him. He responds. I stay with him while his pleasure grows. Where is my fear? I don't recognize myself. And I like it. I take him. No words necessary.

We make love for what seems like hours. I melt into sensation after sensation. My body opens to Chris. To all that he is. I open and I open.

"You can still surprise me," Chris says later, when I come back from the bathroom.

I can still surprise myself, I think.

I smile in the dark.

And then it goes away, and I *get caught up,* as Pema Chödrön so lovingly puts it.

In Tibetan Buddhism, it is called *shenpa,* or attachment. In my case, I get attached to a way of being. Feeling. Experiencing. To a way of knowing myself. To my experience with Chris in the dark of night. To the total loss of inhibition. The openness. The animality. To *I want this* incarnate.

A girl could get used to such a thing. But what, then, when it leaves? Deserts you? When you can't find it? When it has gone far away? Perhaps to a remote island somewhere in the Pacific. On vacation, sipping Mai Tai's on some white Polynesian sandy beach. Nude. Totally naked, half-way across the planet.

Come back! I yell and scream at the top of my lungs. *Don't abandon me so quickly. I need you. I want you. I need to* want.

But today, the very next day, the smell of my love does not ignite heat in my belly. The faded, used up t-shirt with the stretched collar from so many sunscreen applications pushes me away. I am lost, in a sea of confusion and disgust. At myself, for being this kind of me again. At him, for being this kind of him.

As my hard-won, worldly identity returns, the crusty protection that guards my tender heart grows back.

I will not be undone so easily, it says.

At the cold edge of my tender, warm heart, I find a balled fist standing at the center of the ring, ready to fight, masking its fear of dissolution with the bold resistance to its death.

Why must this crust built to protect me from harm lash out and cause hurt before it is able to let go? Why must I bruise us both before I arrive ready once more at the doorstep of love? Why must my worldly identity lose its hold for me to enter fully into love?

Am I crazy?

You don't have to work so hard for love...

⚬

In the afternoon, the softening comes, surprisingly, on its own. Like honey on browning slices of apple at Rosh Hashanah. A cool mountain stream on swollen feet. Two doves huddling on the branch of an oak tree in the chill of early spring.

He touches me, and I do not wince. My body does not instinctively reject the warmth of his palm or the gentle probe of his fingers. The icy shores of my banks have begun to recede, melt back into the turgid waters.

He comes up behind me, puts his arms around my front to rest below my navel. I sink into him. We are dancing now, our own subtle dance, moving again toward union. We do this dance while one of Lillian's new caregivers waits to be fingerprinted in the Odessa County

Clerk's office. While he and Lillian head home, Chris and I explore the adjacent county.

As we walk through the moss-covered nineteenth century graves in the cemetery next to an old church off the side of the road, Chris's hand gently grazes mine. Our touch a slow waltz toward each other through time and space.

"People died young in the 1800s," I say, as we carefully read each gravestone.

"Valerie, aged nine-and-half-years and sixteen days. 1823," he reads.

"Husband, aged forty-two years. 1842," I read.

What kind of life did Husband who died in 1842 know? Surely life was harder then. Losing a child or a spouse, common. Did Husband have time to learn how to love?

Do we?

Is one lifetime ever enough?

We are graced with so much more time these days, I think as I notice the thick, old stand of white pine that protects this sacred place.

I don't want to waste it being shut down to love.

૦ૐ

Oh, the ache.

Once again, I dupe myself into thinking I can stay open forever more. I am caught up. Attached. More *shenpa.* I fall into the trap that I can hold onto *I want this.* This delicious state of being open to love.

I want to be *permanently* changed. I am sure I have discovered a primordial truth. But holding on to being open makes me suffer. I want so much to be feeling something I am not. The further I get from this state of openness the more wrong I feel, the more I hate myself and what currently is.

I am disgraced. A fruitless tree with a fungus.

I will wait until I want again, I think. While I wait, a pervasive anxiety hangs in the air and courses through my veins.

Sitting in Joel's chair, I call myself a survivor of sexual abuse.

"Is that really the word you want to use?" he asks.

A tall upright fan is blowing wisps of hair gently across my face. I shift in my chair and let the rest of my hair down. Pull it all to one side into a temporary twist.

This anxiety is so familiar to me. To my daily life. To the dance Chris and I do to ready ourselves to make love. The way it abates once the walls come down. The way it returns when the walls come back.

You don't have to work so hard for love.

But I have tasted the *I want this* so fully, that I want this; *I want this.* I have lost my taste for coming together while we are both still spinning in opposite spirals, lost the will to force or cajole myself to open.

I will wait until I want again, I decide. But the wait has become excruciating. I have created a storyline, and it is making me suffer.

What would it be like to free myself from this particular suffering? I wonder.

When the aftermath of our union settles and the whirlwind of life picks up, fear creeps in under the door. Slowly at first, then with increasing speed and force.

My body speaks. An unknowable danger is present. It is formless but a worthy rival. I must prepare myself for it could attack at any moment.

Meanwhile, there is no enemy in rational sight. Clear skies all the way to the horizon, and still the fear persists. This is the state of a body that remembers a fundamental uncertainty even when the mind does not. Living with this tormented state, a lifetime of nameless fear, begs the question, *Can I call myself a survivor?*

When a forty-eight-year-old woman lives, coexists, learns how to cope, survive, and thrive with this almost constant unseen torment, she is allowed to call herself a survivor.

How do you learn to relax into your own cycles of desire when they don't match those of your intimate partner, and you have been taught they are supposed to or you are wrong?

"We don't own this body. We don't even own this mind," Joel says as he looks at me with ferocious intensity. "We can take care of it, but it doesn't belong to us."

I can't change what is in my DNA or what was done to my body and my soul before I can remember it, but I am responsible to what arises now.

Can I allow myself to feel the absence of desire without adding judgment? Without attaching a story of inadequacy or injustice? Can I learn to notice the ancient pressure to perform, the desire to feel something that isn't present, then relax and move on? Can I do this just as I can allow myself to feel the intensity of my wanting when it is present and then, move on?

Can I learn to let go and be with what is?

೦ಇ

I had hoped in writing this memoir, in living this healing process, in exploring this constant and recurring theme in my life, that I could somehow surpass it, be permanently changed in such a way that it would no longer rear its ugly face. That I would discover the cure-all and that anyone who read my story would then have access to it as well.

In *Taking the Leap*, Pema Chödrön teaches us the wisdom of staying with the "energy of uncomfortable emotions." By staying with what is, even when it is tremendously uncomfortable, we "change base metal into gold."

> You don't get rid of the base metal—it isn't thrown out and replaced by gold. Instead, the crude metal is itself the source of the precious gold.

> There is nothing to get rid of. Never was.

Pema goes on to refer to the peacock who, by eating poison, makes its tail feathers "become more brilliant and glowing."

The poison is within me. Every time I push it away, feign its nonexistence, avoid, and turn my back, I am not only creating more suffering for myself (and others), but also getting rid of what is needed for my own transformation. This ugly truth, this inner scourge, this pain, this fear, this relentless disfigurement, it is the *Materia prima*. It is the heart and the richness of the bumpy journey toward liberation. Without it, there *is* no getting there.

Can I use my hurt as an ingredient of liberation rather than try to cast it away from my journey?

Chapter Thirteen

And So It Continues . . .

Images of our yearly Adirondack island getaway begin interrupting my thoughts.

"I can't wait to go," I tell Chris. "I'm so excited."

But wait we must. There is much to do before we can escape the world and canoe across the deserted pond to Rock Island—the name we have come to call it due to the long granite beach that extends like a welcome hand into the fresh waters of the small lake.

It is the last week of August. Life has been a whirlwind since our return from the Iberian Peninsula. Trips to Maine for Chris's yearly family reunion and New York for my stepson's wedding. An extended visit from my ex-husband, his partner, and her sons from France. Fullness and family. So much so that by the time we're on the other side of it all, I have all but forgotten the trip that awaits us on the cusp of a new season.

Now, we have packed the car and hoisted the canoe onto the roof rack. Paddles and tent, tarp and blow-up mattress are each tucked neatly between canvas bags filled with cast iron, toilet paper, and dry and wet goods. All that we need for five days on our secluded island fits trimly in the back of our car. We are off. Our annual Adirondack adventure has begun.

The mood in the silver Honda Fit is high as my bare feet find their usual spot on the dashboard. Chris looks over at me. I hold his gaze.

We are silent. We smile. A familiar knot winds almost imperceptibly in my gut.

These trips away are magnificent and challenging. The sudden absence of the boundaries of daily life can leave me groping in midair. A dense need for some sort of protection for my body, Little Me, and that which is vulnerable and feels unsafe.

We have been here so many times. The start of every getaway Chris and I have ever taken is tinged with this fear of free fall followed by a maddening need for control. Very soon into our relationship, I learned to give it voice, and Chris learned to respect it. The mere act of acknowledging this deep, wordless historical knot begins its unraveling. And so, as I open the foil of my breakfast bagel sandwich, I remind Chris of this aspect of myself. He nods, eyes on the road. This nod defends my need to be able to say *no* before I can say *yes*. A subtle caress touches me inside as I take a bite of breakfast and settle in for the ride.

α

The call of the loons greets us as we make our first trip down to the sandy beach, arms loaded.

Loons mate for life and return each year to the same spot to spawn and safely raise their kin. A couple calls from somewhere on the pond to welcome us. The water level is high this year. Small and large broken sticks and wet leaves, Nature's debris, litter the small swath of sand at the top of the beach. We fill every nook and cranny of the canoe and glide, bloated, across the calm surface of the water. Though it is just the end of August, the maple trees have begun to change color. Crimson red outlines the silhouette of trees that respond to the call to turn that comes from deep within the forest.

As we paddle across the pond, our eyes search the waterline for signs of the loons.

"Look, there, 11:00."

Two loons bob in the water ahead, to guide us to our beloved island. We paddle into the slow western movement of the sun, squinting into its rays as they reflect across the wide surface of the gentle waves.

"Remember the year it started pouring when we got here? There were two rainbows."

"Yeah. And two loons."

Our time here would not be the same without the loons. Each day when I wake, I walk the short dirt path lined with low bush blueberries down to the granite rock beach. There, I sit and wait for the loons while Chris makes coffee with the small Italian coffee maker. The morning sun kisses my face.

Invariably they come. They are curious creatures. I hear them first, as the male calls out to the female.

"Where are you?" he croons. A timeless loneliness invades my bones.

"I am here. I am here," she replies as they round the southside of our small island. They are fishing, making frequent dives below the water. Each time they resurface, they have moved eastward, toward a part of the pond that extends beyond three other islands set up for camping in this part of the State Forest.

"Here's your coffee."

Chris settles down next to me on a canoe cushion. Our backs lean against a small boulder covered in green and brown lichen. The morning sun warms us after the cool temperatures of the night. I take off a layer of clothing to get closer to its heat.

It is day three on the island. I have moved through my initial resistance to being cut off from the swirl of humanity and man-made reality. As I sit on the rock, I am content with the rhythm of the island. The slow movement through the day. The way time unfolds. The long

187

silences, listening to the wind, watching the maple leaves turn. It is a time to deeply reflect within.

We eat breakfast: cast-iron cooked bacon, potatoes, and French toast with fresh peaches cut up on the side. Everything tastes better on the island. We take our time as the wind kicks up from the west. I drink my coffee slowly, leave a few sips at the bottom.

We have taken off our clothes and laid out our beach towels. We lie outstretched on the rock. I am drawn to the sweet blush of copper in Chris's pubic hair. I touch it. I linger. His body responds. I want to smell him. Taste him. I take him into my mouth, touch his chest, his shoulders, his neck. He tastes me in return. A noisy seaplane circles overhead. Then another. Chris stops and curses them. I don't mind. Let them circle. Let them watch. Who are we but part of Nature?

All of a sudden, Nature is too much. The elements too strong. As we begin to make love on the beach I am overcome. Things are moving too fast.

"I need to stop," I say, feeling the curse of that hard-to-define something that holds me back from brute surrender.

"Okay."

And we do.

And so, our day begins. We spend the next ten hours journeying within side-by-side. I am drawn to pen and paper. Chris to something else. Now and then, we look at each other and laugh, share a vision, a thought, a question.

"Look," I say, as two loons approach.

We watch as a loon flaps and skims half the length of the pond before it manages to lift off and fly. Unlike most birds whose bones are hollow, the loon's bones are solid. This gives them the weight they need to dive to the bottom of lakes and ponds to feed. It also makes it very difficult to fly.

One of the loons appears to be trying to learn to fly. It scurries, sputters, flaps its wings but does not manage to take off. I watch what appears to be a temper tantrum as the loon slaps the water hard with one wing, rises onto its tail, and squawks loudly. It slaps the water again and makes several turns on itself.

It occurs to me that this isn't just any old temper tantrum but the tantrum of life and death. If this loon doesn't learn to fly, it will die here while the rest of its family flies to warmer waters for the winter. I am humbled to tears as I watch the frustrated, scared loon attack the water.

Later, as I tend the fire, I remember the loon. The fire crackles, flames lick at the air as they rise up into the night.

How does this loon's mother feel? I wonder. She knows the fate that awaits her child if it is unable to fly. Can a mother fly to freedom if it means leaving her progeny behind to slowly wither and die?

My heart twists and breaks as I realize I am seeing my own story in that of the loon. The spirits of the flames show me my son, who now sits very much alive in his wheelchair but will most likely die before I do. The path of Duchenne muscular dystrophy is unforgiving. It progresses and unfolds steadily. At every stage, it steals some level of muscular function, some part of life.

In the precise literal sense, my son cannot fly. We went to Spain without him. We come to this island every year without him. Oh, how I would love to have been able to share the beautiful serenity of this place with him over the years, like so many families have done. My own flight often means leaving my son behind. Eventually, I will have to let him go completely.

I sob into the flames at the truth I am witnessing. The truths of Nature can be brutal. Will mother loon sacrifice her own life to stay with her young that may never fly? No.

Should I?

The wet wood steams. Green flame circles the logs above the fiery coals. I know that I must allow myself to live fully, in my body, whether or not my son can. I mustn't allow my son's physical barriers and limitations to hold me back on my own journey. It is clear.

My broken heart raises an enraged fist to the gods.

Why must it be so?

To which, no answer comes.

It simply is.

My heart grieves hard into the night. I awake to the lonesome call of the solitary loon.

ଔ

The next day I am still feeling the power of the visions from the fire. The mournful emotions within my heart burst free. I cry easily and often. I read a poem I have written to Chris about the loon that cannot fly. My wings, too, are heavy. We cry together.

Making love now is easy. It's as if yesterday and my unexpressed grief were standing in the way. We move to the tent, take time to feel, stop, listen. My orgasm is strong, long, and deep. The sobs follow. At first, it is the fact of being penetrated so deeply. Opened so completely. Then, it is the love and loss of my son. Then just loss. Then just the fullness of loss itself.

Later, on the rock beach, I *see* Chris. In the light of this day, he is sweet and soft and easily broken, like me. How did I miss this? How can I for so long have mistook his sometimes brittle assuredness for strength?

His child is showing. Even though perhaps he, himself, cannot see it.

"We need to take this back with us," I say.

He nods, instinctively knowing what I mean.

CB

I have asked Sarah, Psychology and Childhood Development professor at a local university, to meet me for lunch so that we can talk about the book that got her tenure. It is about the impact of incest and sexual abuse on the identity development of four women.

We take our seats at a round wooden table in the midst of the noon brouhaha that is customary at a local eatery. We sit at the center of the bustle of Ithaca residents hurriedly feeding at lunch hour. We sink quietly toward each other, our privacy protected by the constant hum of activity.

Sarah sips milk as she breaks up the baked salmon on her plate. I tell her how much I loved her book. I ask if she chose the topic of sexual abuse because she had been abused or because of her commitment to feminism. It was the latter. Sarah ran groups for female survivors for ten years before she went back to Yale to pursue her doctorate. These women's stories broke her heart, made her hate men for a while. She held them close, was changed, and made better by their stories of survival and resilience.

Her doctoral thesis—a study based on statistics surrounding family patterns in divorce—was bland in comparison to these women's truths.

"They weren't paying for PhDs on this topic back then."

When her thesis was complete, she burned it.

"My heart was with those women. I got back to that work as soon as I could. I volunteered and continued running groups while I was teaching."

Eight years in, encouraged by colleagues, she got a paid stipend to take a semester off from teaching and write her book.

"I'm getting emotional now," she says as she puts down her milk. Her eyes begin to tear up, "Those women were the most courageous people I have ever met."

Her blue eyes glaze over as the tears fall onto her cheeks. She wipes them away.

"One nice thing about being a woman is that you can cry in public," she says.

"I especially related to Chapter One," I say. The first chapter focuses on sexual abuse that happens in the first year of life. The "pre-memory" phase. At the time she wrote the book, in the late 1990s, the idea of "retrieved memories" was still under debate. Mostly academic men who had never experienced sexual abuse refuted the theory. It wasn't until male veterans' experience of "flashbacks" or memories the psyche has repressed because they were too painful were acknowledged that women's "flashbacks" of sexual trauma were more readily recognized.

"There should be a national holiday every year for abused women," she says.

I let her know why I found Chapter One so compelling.

"It affirms so much of my own experience."

I tell her a little bit about what I am in the process of writing and ask if she would consider being one of my readers.

"I would be honored," she says.

We talk about Latoya, one of the women she interviewed whose story shows up in the book. Latoya's story of incest and sexual abuse is horrific. Her mother was an alcoholic who knew her husband, Latoya's stepfather, was abusing Latoya and did nothing to stop it. In fact, she even held her daughter down one day while he raped her. Latoya was removed from the home and her stepfather went to jail for three years. Latoya was later raped by the captain of the football team in high school. While Latoya's coping strategy was to keep to herself, reject others, and immerse herself in books, she later connected with a teacher who saw her potential. She went on to advocate for children who, like herself, found themselves moving from foster home to foster home, often as mistreated and neglected as they had once been in their family of origin.

Latoya eventually found love. Hers was truly a story of profound resiliency.

"That's what I wanted to feature in my book. Not the stereotypical notion of the lives children of sexual abuse go on to live."

"What stereotype is that?" I ask.

"The one where they are forever broken. I wanted to share the story of their ability to bounce back, find love, and create meaning in their lives. Just like you have done."

"A writing friend says I have to heal this all the way. I don't know if that's possible. What do you think?"

"I think that it is something that will always be with you, always be a part of you, but that it doesn't have to guide your life. You can learn to live with it, and still build the life you want."

I notice the clock on the wall. It's almost time for me to leave.

"I have to go in a minute," I say, "but I want to thank you for your work, your dedication, for this important book and for your time with me."

We stand. We hug. She wraps her arms around my shoulders and hugs me tight.

"I'm headed to see my therapist now," I say.

"That sounds like the perfect thing," she replies.

CB

"Things are different now," I say.

"How so?" Joel asks.

"I left something on the island."

"What?"

"Or maybe I brought something back."

Joel waits, seated across from me in the puffy chair.

"I *saw* him. I saw his vulnerability. We both became totally naked on the island."

"Wonderful," he claps.

Epilogue

According to Levine, the human organism is preprogrammed to heal. Each time the body releases trauma, it restores goodness.

While writing this memoir, deeply visiting, allowing, investigating, feeling, and, ultimately, releasing the stories of trauma still lingering in the shadows of my body, heart, and mind moved me progressively toward wholeness. The work is never done. This pulsation toward wholeness continues. Indeed, it never stops.

In *Chakra Yoga*, Anodea Judith writes, "Awakening is a gradual realization of an integrated wholeness in everything, a deeper access to who you really are, and a persistent presence of grace."

How do I *know* I am healing?

I feel it in my increasing capacity to receive my mother's love. In my growing willingness to receive her touch. In my crescive trust in her absolute desire to see me flourish, even when she's still sometimes too caught up in her own challenges to fully see me.

I see this healing in the robust way my body seeks intimate contact with my husband. In the way I open more easily to his touch and laugh more frequently at his humor. In the way I give less and less energy to the part of me that sees him as dangerous, a threat, or as someone who wishes to do me harm.

I know this healing in the swelling steadiness I find in myself, a steadiness I, and others, can lean into and glean solace from when times get tough.

This healing allows tears of grief to flow more freely from deep within my belly without shame. To more readily embrace Little Me when she gets angry or sad or feels neglected.

This healing moves me toward the available friend, the neighbor who has time to talk, and those who are truly interested and want to listen—even as the part of me that still seeks the approval of those who will never show me love tries to tug me away.

I fall.

I get up.

And I grow into the beauty that *being* in love brings.

Recommended Reading

Author's Note: The following list of books I found to be helpful on my journey to wholeness.

ॐ

Trauma

Stephen Levine, *Waking the Tiger: Healing Trauma.* North Atlantic Books, 1997.

Bessel van der Kolk, MD, *The Body Keeps the Score: Brain, Mind and Body in the Healing of Trauma.* Penguin Books, 2014.

Matthew Sanford, *Waking: A Memoir of Trauma and Transcendence.* Rodale, 2006.

David Emerson and Elizabeth Hopper, PhD, *Overcoming Trauma through Yoga: Reclaiming Your Body.* North Atlantic Books, 2011.

Pat Ogden, Kekuni Minton, Clare Pain, *Trauma and the Body: A Sensorimotor Approach to Psychotherapy.* W.W. Norton and Company, 2006.

Pat Ogden and Janina Fisher, Sensorimotor Psychotherapy: Interventions for Trauma and Attachment. W.W. Norton and Company, 2015.

Self-Help

Brené Brown, *Braving the Wilderness: The Quest for True Belonging and the Courage to Stand Alone*. Vermillion, 2017.

Regena Thomashauer, *Pussy: A Reclamation*. Hay House, 2016.

Love and Intimacy

Gina Ogden, PhD, *The Return of Desire: A Guide to Rediscovering Your Sexual Passion*. Trumpeter Books, 2008.

Nicole Daedone, *Slow Sex: The Art and Craft of the Female Orgasm*. Grand Central Life & Style, 2011.

John Gray, PhD, *Mars and Venus in the Bedroom: A Guide to Lasting Romance and Passion*. Harper Torch, 2001.

David Schnarch, PhD, *Passionate Marriage*: *Keeping Love & Intimacy Alive in Committed Relationships*. Owl Books, 1997.

Gabrielle Roth with John Loudon, *Maps to Ecstasy: A Healing Journey for the Untamed Spirit*. Nataraj Publishing, 1998.

Yoga Philosophy and Practice

Pema Chödrön, *When Things Fall Apart: Heart Advice for Difficult Times*. Shambhala Publications, 1997.

Living Beautifully with Uncertainty and Change. Shambhala Publications, 2012.

The Places that Scare You: A Guide to Fearlessness in Difficult Times. Shambala Publications, 2001.

Sally Kempton, *Awakening Shakti: The Transformative Power of the Goddesses of Yoga*. Sounds True, 2013.

Meditation for the Love of it: Enjoying Your Own Deepest Experience. Sounds True, 2011.

Anodea Judith, *Chakra Yoga.* Llwellyn Publications, 2017.

Eastern Body, Western Mind. Celestial Arts, 2004.

Yongey Mingyur Rinpoche with Helen Tworkov, *In Love With the World: A Monk's Journey through the Bardos of Living and Dying.* Bluebird, 2019.

Phakyab Rinpoche and Sofia Stil-Rever, *Meditation Saved My Life: A Tibetan Lama and the Healing Power of the Mind.* New World Library, 2017.

Christopher D. Wallis, *Tantra Illuminated: The Philosophy, History, and Practice of a Timeless Tradition.* Mattamayura Press, 2013.

Easwaran Eknath, *The Bagavad Gita.* Nilgiri Press, 2007.

Don Miguel Ruiz, *The Mastery of Love: A Practical Guide to the Art of Relationship.* Amber-Allen Publishing, Inc., 1999.

Memoir

Eve Ensler, *In the Body of the World: A Memoir of Cancer and Connection.* Picadore, 2013.

Anne Lamott, *Bird by Bird: Some Instructions on Writing and Life.* Anchor Books, 1995.

Anne Dillard. *The Writing Life.* Harper, 1989.

Dani Shapiro, *Hourglass: Time, Memory, Marriage.* Knopf, 2017.

Inheritance: A Memoir of Genealogy, Paternity, and Love. Knopf, 2019.

Darcey Steinke, *Flash Count Diary: Menopause and the Vindication of Natural Life.* Sarah Crichton Books, 2019.

Eloise Ristad, *A Soprano on Her Head: Right-side-up Reflections on Life and Other Performances.* Real People Press, 1982.

Poetry

Mary Oliver, *Why I Wake Early.* Beacon Press, 2004.

A Thousand Mornings. Penguin Books, 2012.

Thirst. Beacon Press, 2006.

David Whyte, *Consolations: The Solace, Nourishment and Underlying Meaning of Everyday Words.* Many Rivers Press, 2018.

Daniel Ladinsky, *A Year with Hafiz: Daily Contemplations.* Penguin Books, 2011.

Rumi translated by Maryan Mafi and Azima Melita Kolin. *Rumi's Little Book of Life: The Garden of the Soul, the Heart, and the Spirit.* Hampton Roads, 2012.

Rilke translated by Anita Barrows and Joanna Macy. *Rilkes Book of Hours.* Riverhead Books, 2005.

Other

Peter Wohlleben. *The Hidden Life of Trees.* William Collins, 2016.

Daniel Floor, PhD. *Ancestral Medicine: Rituals for Personal and Family Healing.* Bear & Co., 2017.

Acknowledgments

Writing a book is no solo journey. It's a long, often endless seeming path with helpers all along the way. My first help came from a wise woman who said, "You're writing a memoir? You're going to need a therapist, an editor, and regular bodywork." I quickly put together my team!

Thank you Jeff, Hilary, and Trish. A special thanks to my first readers. They read my work in the naïve early stage when I thought my book was finished. Krissy and Kat, you are saints. Randy, you helped me to see that my work was still rough and needed the skilled eye of someone who knows the trade. Nancy, we found each other at just the right moment. You are the good witch who helped me find my way on my own yellow brick road. It's history from here.

Finally, there is my biggest fan, my mother, and my stalwart companion in life, Chris. You both make all the difference.

Made in the USA
Monee, IL
16 August 2021

74940504R10125